Life with Mollie but Really It's All About Me

Life with Mollie but Really It's All About Me

Sherry Turner

This is a memoir and a true story based on the recollection of the author. Some of the names and places have been changed to protect the privacy of individuals in the story. The timeline may be slightly altered or compressed. The back-stories are related as closely as possible to the way Mollie told them, and in many cases are documented by letters or photographs. The chapter titles are all song titles as a tribute to Mollie's ability to remember tunes and lyrics to almost every song she ever heard.

A Portion of the Proceeds from the Sale of this Book
Will be donated to The Alzheimer's Association

ISBN: 1535581247
ISBN 13: 9781535581240
Library of Congress Control Number: 2016914076
CreateSpace Independent Publishing Platform
North Charleston, South Carolina

For Jennifer and Brian
My Real Life Heroes

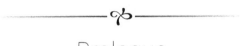

Prologue

Mollie is making her way down our long, winding, pine needle driveway to check the mail. This is the third time today she has done this, and each time she has asked me if she needs a sweater. Each time, I have tried patiently to explain that it is summertime in Florida and that she doesn't need one. Mollie remembers none of this…Mollie has Alzheimer's disease.

After she leaves, I take advantage of a quiet moment to go to my office and check my e-mail. I also get on *Facebook,* and before I realize, almost a half-hour has passed. I return to the family room and look down the driveway to check on Mollie. She is nowhere in sight. Where could she have gone? I check her room and the kitchen…No Mollie. I run out of the house and toward the mailbox, calling her name.

As I hurry toward the road, I check places where she might be. We have a garage that Bob built for storage. He designed it to look like an old-fashioned country store and gas station. He must have done a pretty good job because Mollie tells people that we used to have an old man who ran it, but we fired him for sleeping on the job. This, of course, is untrue.

It has a covered front porch with a rocking chair, and sometimes Mollie will stop and sit in the rocker, while she opens the mail. My husband Bob and his father share the same name, so

Mollie thinks the mail is for her and her deceased husband. She is not on the porch today.

We have a small citrus grove on one side of the drive. Mollie likes to walk through it to check the ripeness of the fruit when in season. She is not there either.

When I reach the mailbox on the dirt road, I look in both directions, but there is no sign of her. I am beginning to feel a bit panicked. What if she went out on the road? What if she gets run over? I had read about people with her condition, wandering or trying to return to their old homestead, but Mollie had been with us for over a year and had never done anything like that. Where could she be?

I rush over to Bob's shop and explain what has happened. He jumps in the golf cart to go down the road toward the highway. (I don't tell him how long I neglected to check on her and I feel guilty for that.) I head for the dock on the lake behind our house. Mollie loves to sit on the dock with us in the early evening to watch the colors of the sunset. I don't think she would go there alone because she can't swim and is afraid of water...but what if she did?

My heart is pounding a staccato beat that hurts my ears and I feel almost sick to my stomach. What kind of a caregiver am I? How could I have let this happen? What if she has been run over in the road? What if she has drowned? Why did I leave her alone for so long? This is all my fault.

I think back to when Mollie came to live with us and the visions that I had of being such a wonderful caregiver...

CHAPTER 1

---- ✎ ----

Fly Me to The Moon
Frank Sinatra -- 1964

MY HUSBAND BOB and I are standing at the Orlando airport waiting for the passengers to emerge from the arriving flight concourse. There is a bustling sea of humanity around us: families with children sporting Mickey Mouse ears, weary-looking men in uniform, searching the crowd for their sweethearts, limousine drivers holding up signs with last names printed boldly: Dr. Smith, Callahan Party, Familia Rodriquez. As I look at the throng of faces, I think of how each one has a story, some joyous, some tragic, each unique. Our story is just beginning.

Bob and I have spent the last week in a flurry of activity getting ready for this moment, which has been a long time in the making. I am wondering if I will be up to the task ahead. My 88-year old mother-in-law, Mollie Elizabeth Bennett Turner, will be arriving shortly with my husband's sister Mary. Mollie believes she is coming for a visit, but in reality she is coming to live with us permanently.

For many people, this thought would bring dread to their hearts, but "Mom" has been my best friend for the past 43 years of marriage to her son. She has always treated me more like a daughter than a daughter-in-law. She has never offered unsolicited advice or criticized anything I did. She has always seen my side of the story in any disagreement that Bob and I had. In short, she is the perfect mother-in-law.

The complicating issue to this fairy tale is that she now has some form of dementia, possibly Alzheimer's disease. She continued to live in her own home in Tennessee after her husband died, and between the three of them, my sisters-in-law have been keeping her out of too much trouble. But now, the oldest sister Mary, who is legally blind and has moved in with Mollie, wants to return to Texas and reclaim a bit of the life she had lived there. Kathy and Kristie, the two younger girls have been sharing in the task of Mom's care. They've been doing all the shopping and doctors' visits that Mary cannot do because of her blindness. They are burned out, while Bob and I have been living a beautiful, carefree life of retirement in Florida. Now, it's our turn.

As we wait anxiously, my thoughts turn to the last time we visited Mom in Tennessee about six months ago. She had always been a happy, optimistic person with an easy going personality and she remained extremely sweet. I remember thinking that the girls were exaggerating the pressures that caring for her placed on them. After all, she didn't even live with Kathy or Kristie. They had to look in on her daily, spend a little time with her and shop for her. Mary did live with her, but everyone had noticed that Mary had become rather inflexible since she lost her eyesight to macular degeneration. I really believed that with a little more laid-back attitude, I could do a better job.

I lost my own mother eight years earlier, and although I felt I had been a good daughter and done all the things I should have,

I never did them with a happy heart. There had always been a wedge in my relationship with my mother. I was embarrassed by her. I remember when I was a teenager, I would insist that she let me out of the car three blocks from school so that the kids wouldn't see her flaming red-dyed hair. One would have thought those feelings would have abated in adulthood, but for me they never did. Waiting for Mollie today, I still feel those familiar pangs of guilt. Perhaps this will give me a chance to redeem myself!

I picture myself taking her to concerts and shopping, ever patient, other people watching me and thinking, "That woman is such a wonderful caregiver, so gentle and attentive; what a lucky mother to be treated so kindly." So, as I stand in the crowded airport, I am filled with hope and anticipation; and I feel as if God is granting me a second chance to be a kinder person than I was to my own mother.

I am roused from my reverie by a parade of people beginning to emerge from the arrival gates. Bob spots them first and says, "There they are, behind that man in the plaid shirt. See, Mary's pushing Mom in a wheelchair. Why in the world didn't she get a porter? How in the hell can she maneuver that thing when she can hardly see?" He shakes his head. "I don't get it, she is one stubborn cookie."

I am shocked to see how frail Mary has become, and her complexion has a decidedly yellow hue. She can't see us waving at them, but Mom does, and the look of relief on her face almost breaks my heart. I was concerned that she might not recognize us. I had been torturing myself over how I would handle it if she didn't know us.

She is dressed in black slacks and a little black-and-white plaid jacket. Her gray coat is on her lap with a small carry-on bag. I can see that someone has gone to a lot of trouble styling her soft gray curls and I realize that although the girls will be relieved to have her living with us, they will also miss her.

"Oh, Bobby and Sherry," she says, "Where have you been? We've been lost forever. I was sooo afraid."

"Oh, Mom, for heaven's sake," Mary barks. "I told you we weren't lost, we've just flown down here on an airplane."

"Well, you might have been on an airplane, but I was in a big dark tunnel and I haven't seen any of you for hours."

Mary shakes her head and rolls her eyes. She is holding her body stiffly, and I get the message that it has been a stressful flight for her as well. She is about to say something else, but stops when Bob gently takes over the wheelchair.

I give Mary a big hug and hook my arm in hers to help guide her through the airport. She snatches her arm away. "I'm not crippled, and I can see well enough to make out where I'm going." I recoil at her tone, and she says more gently, "I know you're just trying to help, but I need my independence." Then she adds, "I sure am happy to be here though."

Mary goes with Bob to get the car and have a smoke. I watch their backs as they walk to the escalator, and it strikes me that they have a similar gait. Mary is seven years younger than Bob and as a little girl, she idolized him and always copied him when they were kids. He was her hero, and I guess some things never change.

I wait with Mom at baggage claim. She has asked me at least six times, "Where are we going now? Are we in New Jersey? Am I going to see my mother?" Her mother has been dead for over 30 years, and I feel my prior optimism flag just a little.

On the ride home, Mom is tired and doesn't ask too many questions. Mary is tired too, but she says several times that she needs another cigarette, and although unspoken, I know that she could use a drink as well. Come to think of it, so could I. It has been quite a day for us all. I think back to the final event that made us realize that Mom needed to move in with us.

We received a frantic call from Kristie that she was missing. Mary had been visiting her children for a few days. Mom had taken the car to the grocery store and couldn't remember how to get home. They didn't find her for hours. She drove until she ran out of gas and got out and started walking down a treacherous stretch of highway. A policeman picked her up and called home. My God, the girls didn't think she even had keys to the car anymore, but somehow she found a spare set. That was a wake-up call for us all.

I can't help thinking that a new chapter in our lives is about to begin. Bob and I live in our dream home in Florida. It's an older home, built in 1952 before air conditioning, so every bedroom is a separate wing with its own bathroom and windows on all sides. The view from all of the rooms is spectacular, with one of two lakes visible from every vantage point. This creates a very private and intimate feeling.

The ancient oaks on the property are draped with Spanish moss and the huge stately long-leaf pines remind me of sentinels protecting us from harm. The landscaping directly around the house is well-manicured, but the balance of the five acres is heavily wooded and also contains a small citrus grove. This makes it a home for many varieties of birds and butterflies and an occasional critter. We have seen raccoons, possums, foxes, armadillos and even a bear. There are always a lot of squirrels, sand hill cranes, pileated woodpeckers, cardinals and many seasonal visitors. It's our version of paradise, and I knew Mom would love it.

When we found she would be coming to live with us, we converted one of the bedrooms and baths into her own little suite. We took out one of the twin beds, put in an easy chair and television, and gussied it up with some of her personal things. We put photographs around the room of Mollie's husband, Bob Senior, and all of her children, grandchildren, and great grandchildren. We also hung several of the watercolors that she had painted many years ago. The painting of her childhood home in Smyrna, Delaware had a place of honor over her bed and the tulip painting that she had named *Languid Lovelies* hung on the opposite wall.

Mollie had always loved looking at her old photographs, which the girls had sent with some of her other things prior to her arrival. I had gathered them together and placed them in a pretty wicker basket on top of the cedar chest, so that they would be readily available for her to enjoy. It had been fun fixing up the room, and I was anticipating how much she would appreciate it.

Mom and I follow Bob as he carries her suitcase into the room. She moves to the dresser and picks up the photograph of her husband. It was taken at Kristie's wedding and he is dressed in a tuxedo and seated with his hands folded in his lap. He was a very handsome man, even at seventy years old. Mom caresses his face as Bob and I watch her.

"Well, Bobby, I guess you got your good looks from your dad," she says, and I notice she has tears in her eyes.

"Daddy was always better looking than I am." He replies.

She keeps walking around the room, touching this and that, but not saying anything more. I am beginning to worry that she doesn't like it.

Finally she turns with a big smile on her face, "Why this is the prettiest bedroom I ever saw and I think those paintings are some of my water colors," she says. This is a good omen, and my spirits soar.

Bob goes out to help Mary with her things, and I unpack enough of Mom's suitcase to find her toothbrush and nightgown. She seems exhausted and is uncharacteristically quiet.

"Would you like a little snack or do you just want to go to bed?" I ask.

"I am tired, and since you have gone to so much trouble already, getting this hotel room and all, I guess I'll just go to sleep."

I don't bother to correct her. I help her out of her clothes and into her nightgown. Then, I show her to the bathroom, where I have laid out her toiletries and turned on a night light. I hope she's not too confused. I wait for her to come out and when I help her under the covers, she promptly starts to say her prayers. When she has finished asking God's blessings on us all, she rolls over and mumbles, "I don't know why exactly, but I feel like crying." I realize how confused she is, and I feel the same way.

The next morning when I get up, Bob is reading the paper in his recliner, and Mary is on the screened-in porch smoking a cigarette and drinking a cup of coffee. He looks over the top of the paper and gives me a smile. I pinch the sock on his big toe as I pass his chair, a little ritual that I have developed. I peek in on Mom and she is in the same position she was in when I checked on her during the night. I pour myself a cup of coffee and go out to join Mary.

"Did you sleep well?" I ask. "Yesterday was pretty rough for you."

"Yeah, but it wasn't too bad. Mom was fairly cooperative, although she didn't have a clue as to what was happening." She shakes her head and continues in an almost angry tone. "I know you think this will be easy for you, but you really have no idea. She will drive you crazy. The worst thing is the constant barrage of questions and the repetition. It just saps everything out of you."

"I know it's been hard on you, and you've handled it really well in spite of your blindness," I say

"Adjusting to my loss of sight was easy compared to seeing Mom like this, but you'll find out soon enough. Listen, there are a few things you should know. She usually doesn't get up until sometime around noon. If you're smart, you'll take advantage of that to get things done, because once she's up, she'll want to help you with everything, and she can't actually do anything. That sounds mean, but if you let her help you, it'll take you twice as long and frustrate the shit out of you. I know you don't believe me, but you'll see.

"And another thing, you have to bathe her because she doesn't wash herself properly. She can't remember what parts she has washed, and she'll pitch a fit when you suggest a bath. She'll tell you she already took one. Don't believe her, and don't bathe her every day; once or twice a week is plenty."

For some reason she is getting worked up as she tells me this stuff, and I am thinking that I will certainly bathe her more often than that, but I'm not about to say so. She crushes her cigarette out abruptly in the ashtray and immediately shakes another one from the pack.

I'm uncomfortable and confused at Mary's anger. I wonder if she feels guilty about leaving her Mother. She has really done a good job under less than ideal circumstances. I'd like to tell her that, but I'm afraid to. She's very hard to read, and I don't want to appear condescending.

"Now Mary, I'll do just fine, you don't have to worry about anything. Besides you'll be here to give me some on-the-job training for a couple of weeks, won't you?"

I'm surprised when she says, "I'm afraid not. I'd like to leave tomorrow morning if you don't mind. Can you or Bobby drive me to the bus station? I'm sorry but the bus to Texas leaves Ocala at five o'clock in the morning."

"Of course we can, but I wish you could stay a little longer." The look she gives me tells me not to pursue this subject. I go in the house for another cup of coffee. Mary remains on the porch.

I tell Bob her plans later that day and ask him to talk to her. He says that we should not interfere with her choices. She has her own way of doing things, and nobody is going to change her. Bob had previously tried to coax her into flying back to Texas, but she wouldn't hear of it. She said it was a waste of money, and besides, she liked the people she met on the bus. I knew she had plans to move in with Carlos, her old boyfriend, and I wondered what her living conditions would be. From what she had told me, there were several families living in his household. Mary has always been the rebel, and there is nothing that we can say or do to change her.

As I hug her good-bye the next morning, I am sad that she seems so angry with life. For all her gruffness and bravado, I know the gentle side of Mary, and I love her. I remember when her kids were little and she and Chet were still married. She was such fun to be with. We would sit up playing board games until the wee hours of the morning. There was always so much laughter. Where had that person gone? Bob told me that he plans to give her some money when he puts her on the bus and I know that will help. I can only hope that her new life brings her some happiness.

True to Mary's prediction, I finally go in and wake Mom up at 11:45. She doesn't even ask where Mary is.

CHAPTER 2

—— ❦ ——

Body and Soul
Ella Fitzgerald - 1936

ON THE THIRD day after Mary's departure, as Mollie is sitting in the family room, I realize that she has not yet had a bath

"Mom, why don't you let me help you get a nice bath?" I say.

She looks up with a startled expression. "Oh my goodness, you don't need to do that. I'm pretty sure I took a bath this morning."

I think about what Mary told me. "Well, let's give it a try." I'm trying to be good natured and not blow this whole thing out of proportion. "I'll just get you started. After all, you're not familiar with your bathroom yet. C'mon." I help her up out of the chair and guide her through her room and into her bathroom. She's dragging her feet and barely moving as I close the door behind me.

"Okay, let's get your clothes off and get started." I reach for her blouse, and she jerks away. This is going to be harder than I thought.

"I can bathe myself, and besides, I already did." She starts to cry.

"Oh Mom, please, don't make this hard. You are eighty-eight years old, and you need a little help. That's where I come in.

C'mon now." I pull her top over her head, and I notice that she is shaking, so I pull her close and hug her. Big mistake: Now she's really wailing.

I take her back into the bedroom. "Okay, just sit in your chair for a minute and calm down." I wrap a throw around her shoulders as she sinks into her chair. "I'm going to go into the bathroom and get things ready."

I leave her and try to collect my thoughts. She has to have a bath, and she can't do it herself. She has always been a very modest person, and maybe the thought of being nude in front of me is more than she can bear. This is up to me. I need to show her kindness, and I need to be patient with her. I have to summon "Good Sherry" from deep within. She's in there somewhere, although like some of Sybil's alter egos in the movie, she is frequently in hiding, and "Evil Sherry" seems more likely to make an appearance.

I think about the last hours of my own mother's life. She had always been somewhat needy and although I knew this, "Evil Sherry" seemed to delight in withholding the physical contact I knew she craved. As she lay dying, and I realized it, I couldn't hug her enough. "Good Sherry" was clearly in control, albeit rather late.

I gather my thoughts as I hang the baby-blue robe that Kathy gave Mom on the back of the bathroom door. She loves that robe and always comments about its softness. Maybe its familiarity will be comforting to her. I position the bath chair that Mary sent from Tennessee. It is a chair about half again as wide as a regular chair. It is positioned in the tub so that two of its legs are inside the tub and the other two are outside. This makes it easy for a person to sit down and then lift and swing her legs over and into the tub. It's a great design because it eliminates the possibility of falling while trying to climb in. I check the hand-held shower attachment that Bob has installed for Mollie's use. I make sure I have shampoo, conditioner and body wash along with a wash cloth and plenty of towels at hand.

As I ready things for her bath, I think back to when my two daughters were young and how bathing them was one of my favorite chores. Their chubby little bodies were such a delight to behold. The contrast of their healthy tanned skin against their little white bottoms was a thing of beauty. Youth is so fleeting and I wish I had reveled more in the appreciation for it during my mothering days. Somehow, I don't think bathing Mollie will have the same feel.

When I go back into her bedroom, she is huddled under the throw, and she doesn't look happy. I tune the radio to a station that plays old standards from the thirties and forties. Mollie loves this music and often sings along in perfect pitch, remembering all the words flawlessly. I often wonder why she can remember them so well. Could those types of memories be stored in a different part of her brain?

"Okay, Mom. Everything is ready. Let's just get your drawers off and get this show on the road." I try to cajole her into shedding the rest of her clothes. She starts to cry again, but she pulls off her shoes and socks and I help her with her pants. I'll tackle the undergarments when I get her in the tub. I wrap a towel around her and think how fragile her shriveled body seems to be. "Good Sherry" is touched by her vulnerability.

This is the beginning of a routine that will be repeated several times a week with slight variations for as long as Mollie lives with us.

She almost always cries when I bathe her, but once we get going, I think she actually enjoys it. I usually soap up her hair first, rinse and apply conditioner. While the conditioner is working, I hand her a wash cloth and have her wash her face. By the time, I start washing her back; she has usually stopped crying and is enjoying her bath.

One time I say, "Let's trim your toenails today."

"Oh, let's wait until next time; it will give you something to look forward to," she replies.

Several months later as we are going through our usual bath routine, I get a surprise. We have reached the point in our routine where Mollie needs to wash her private parts. I hand her a soapy wash cloth and she gets busy.

"Now Mom, it's really important that you rinse yourself thoroughly," I say as I hand her the shower wand. "You could be very uncomfortable if you don't rinse all the soap off."

She looks at me sweetly and says, "Sherry, do you know the difference between the lady in church and the lady in the bathtub?"

"No." I reply, as I adjust the temperature of the water.

"Well," she says, with the innocence of a six year old child telling her first "knock-knock" joke.

"The lady in church has hope in her soul, while the lady in the bathtub has soap in..."

She rolls her eyes, and watches me expectantly. When I finally fill in the blanks, we both laugh so heartily, I almost fall in the tub with her.

I can't wait to tell Bob his mother's little joke.

What I am learning through this experience, however, is that in spite of Mollie's pleasant nature and clever quips, the best thing about bathing her is this: After she has been coaxed into the tub, and washed and dried and powdered; and her hair has been blown dry and styled; and she is sitting in her chair in her soft blue robe, eating a cookie and drinking a cup of coffee, I can go out to Bob's workshop, drink a glass of wine with him, and realize that for the next few days, I don't have to do it again.

I also am coming to realize that Mary was right; once or twice a week is enough.

CHAPTER 3

Getting to Know You
Bing Crosby - 1951

ADJUSTING TO MOLLIE'S presence seems easy at first. She is not at all demanding. She is content to sit in her chair in the family room and either watch television or sort through her basket of photographs. Bob takes her for rides around the yard in the golf cart, and she appreciates every bush, bloom or tree.

She raves about every meal I prepare for her, even if it is just a Lean Cuisine. She definitely has a sweet tooth, but I find that if I put the cookie jar out of sight, she won't go looking for it.

At first, she says things that imply that she is only visiting, "Well, you folks are probably getting sick of this old lady by now. I think it's time I went home to see how Daddy is doing without me."

This is poignant on two levels: first of all "Daddy," her husband, passed away two years ago, and secondly, this is now her home. We usually just let those comments slide while assuring her that we love having her with us.

She also can't remember that her mother is no longer living, and she is always wishing that she could come and visit and see all the beautiful flowers. As I recall, her relationship with her family was quite rocky, and they were estranged for years;

but those memories seem to have vanished entirely. She now seems to feel nothing but love and admiration for her mother and father.

One day as she is sitting at the table in the kitchen eating a bowl of Cheerios, and I am rinsing dishes at the sink, she stops eating and asks, "Sherry, do I have a husband?"

I sigh and stop washing the dishes. I dry my hands and walk over to the table, all the while wondering just how to respond. It is very distressing to me to realize that such an important time in her life is gone from her memory. I sit down across from her.

I have read that sometimes in cases of dementia or stroke, different parts of the brain can be trained to take over for the damaged portions. I decide to try and make her dig into her mind for the answer to her question.

"Mom, you were married to the same man for more than sixty years: surely you can remember him. You have a picture of him on your dresser. He was a very good man and quite handsome. Now try to remember who he was."

"It was Bobby Turner, wasn't it? All the girls at school loved him." She gets a little giggly.

"That's right." I'm feeling gratified that this might work. Maybe by confronting these lapses of memory and forcing her to search her mind for the answers, we can turn this around.

"Now try to remember... he went to France during the war and you had a little baby to take care of all by yourself. Who was that little baby?"

"Was it Kathy?"

"No Mom." I try not to feel disappointed. "It was your oldest child, Bobby Turner, Jr."

"Oh, that's right, does he live near here?"

"Mom," I say, not nearly as patiently as a nice person would have, "He lives here with you and me. He's your oldest child, and he's my husband."

"Do I have a husband?" she asks again.

I feel as though someone is inside my body rubbing all of my nerve endings with sandpaper. This is going to be so hard. I pour a little more cereal in Mollie's bowl and rise from the table. She doesn't seem to realize that I haven't answered. She is glancing at the newspaper.

I feel almost physically ill as I walk back to the sink. I also am angry. I think how angry Mary had become as she was explaining Mollie's condition to me. At the time, I had thought that she was angry with Mollie, but now I realize with amazing clarity that she was angry with the disease and how much it had taken from her mother. I feel the same way.

How could something like this have happened to such a wonderful person?

How can Mollie not remember her husband Bob? She has told me the story of their romance more times than I can remember.

Mollie was born December 16, 1917 in Wilmington, Delaware. She was the third child, and her mother developed some kind of infection that kept her in the hospital for some time after the birth. She was originally named Maggie after her maternal grandmother. When Maggie was two years old, her grandmother died, and her mother changed her little girl's name to Mollie. She said it caused her too much grief to call her Maggie and be continually reminded of her dead mother. I always thought that was weird.

I wondered if the little toddler was confused that everyone was now calling her Mollie.

Mollie's father worked at the DuPont chemical plant. It was a local joke that you could always tell what "Uncle Dupie" was cooking by the color of the water in the canals that led to the Delaware River. Mollie remembered her early childhood as quite happy, although times were hard and there was never enough money to go around. Her mother took in sewing to supplement their income, and picked up odd jobs whenever she was able. Mollie remembered going with her mother to pick blueberries for a local farmer and being paid a nickel a quart. Life was simple, but not easy.

Mollie's older sister Vera was always regarded as the pretty one, although she was painfully shy. The oldest child, her brother John, was also quiet and withdrawn. Both of them regarded their younger sister as a pest.

Mollie was a smart girl and when she started high school, she was elected Class Secretary. A young man named Robert Turner was Class President. His father also worked for DuPont, but he was a foreman. His family did not live in company housing like Mollie's did. His mother was a tiny, dynamic woman who somehow managed to always get things for her children that other kids didn't have.

Mollie had a huge crush on Bob, and looking at pictures from his youth, I can see why. He had a beautifully sculpted nose, a head full of glossy black hair and a quiet, kind of sultry demeanor that all the girls found very appealing. When Bob started showing an interest in Mollie, she thought she had died and gone to heaven.

Mollie's mother was not happy with this turn of events. She thought the Turners were uppity. Mollie was a little insecure, and she couldn't believe that Bob had chosen her to be his girlfriend; so when her mother told Mollie that Bob wasn't really interested in her, she believed it.

"Why would he be?" she said. "You have a rear end as big as a cow."

Mollie had always been self-conscious about her weight, and when her mother said this, she ran from the house sobbing. She walked several miles to Bob's house; but when she got there, she kept walking around the block because she couldn't get up the nerve to knock on the door.

Things came to a head several months later. Bob and Mollie had both graduated from high school, and true to her reputation, Bob's mother had figured out a way to get him a car. It was a jalopy to be sure; but nonetheless a car. He invited Mollie to go with him and some friends to the shore for a picnic. As Bob started up the walk to Mollie's front door, her brother John and a couple of friends started heckling him. They started throwing rocks at him, spitting on him and taunting him with names like "rich little mick," "pretty boy" and "Mama's baby." When things began to get physical, Bob pulled a tire iron from underneath the seat, and when John came at him with a pipe, he hit him across the mouth and knocked out several teeth. Mollie jumped in the car, crying, and they drove away in a cloud of dust. Mollie was hysterical, and Bob took her to his house, where his mother calmed her down and said she could stay there for the night and sleep in the room with his two sisters.

Mollie's mother could not get over this. Mollie had stayed away overnight with a boy who had knocked out her son's teeth. She was sure Mollie's reputation had been ruined, and that she had been compromised by that "uppity Turner boy." She sent word that she was no longer welcome in her home.

Mollie had been hired in a clerical position at DuPont right after graduation, and she and a girl she worked with decided to get their own apartment. Mollie's brother filed a lawsuit against Bob for assault and battery.

When the judge in the case found Bob innocent after the facts had been presented, Mollie's brother asked, "What about my teeth?"

To that, the judge responded, "I'm a judge, not a dentist."

I remember Mollie telling me this story many years ago, but now she remembers none of it. The only thing that she now remembers is that her family didn't like Bob because he was Catholic.

CHAPTER 4

— ✎ —

All Alone Am I
Brenda Lee - 1963

BEFORE MOM CAME to live with us, Bob and I had many discussions about how our life would be altered; and although I knew this was true, I felt we were up to the challenge. I had even attended a seminar that Lake County held for "Caregivers." It had been enlightening, but because of Mollie's gentle nature, I really didn't think I would have any of the problems they cautioned us about. I also had never dealt with a person with dementia before. My own mother had been in control of her faculties until the end.

The first part of the seminar dealt with the statistics of Alzheimer's disease. I learned that in Alzheimer's disease, the brain's communication system is impaired. Disturbances or deficiencies in either the structural mechanism (the neurons) or the chemical messengers (the neurotransmitters) can lead to disturbances in behavior, thought or emotion. It is thought that build-ups of a plaque called Amyloid, which is a sticky protein that attaches itself to brain cells, contribute to these disturbances. It is estimated that by the year 2040, fourteen million Americans are expected to have this disease.

I heard horror stories from other caregivers. One older man told us that his wife didn't sleep all night long. If he didn't stay up and watch her, she would turn on the stove or go outside. Sometimes, she would just start breaking things; even things that she had valued. She had become mean and abusive. He was at his wits' end and was considering putting her into a home for dementia patients.

He said sadly, "I took her hand in mine one evening and said, 'Martha, please for the love of God, go to sleep tonight. I really need to get some rest.'"

"She tossed her head like she used to when she was a young, beautiful woman, and said, 'If you can't handle this job they should hire somebody who can.'" I felt sorry for him.

Another woman told the group about her mother-in-law, who was in an Alzheimer's facility. She had been a very active person during her lifetime, but now she was interested in nothing and had become nasty and belligerent. No one wanted to share a room with her; and every time they gave her a new roommate, she would physically beat her up.

The woman had never liked her daughter-in-law, but had managed to keep her feelings under wraps. But now, even that modicum of conduct had disappeared. One day the son came to take his mother out to dinner. His wife had gotten into the back seat so that her mother-in-law could sit up front.

As he helped his mother into her seat, she asked, "Where's your fat-faced wife?"

Her son replied, "Oh, she's in the back seat."

"Well, at least she's quiet for a change," she retorted.

I also learned that at present there were over five million people in the United States suffering from some type of dementia and that Alzheimer's disease is the sixth leading cause of death and the only one out of the top ten for which there is no known cure. In addition, approximately seventy percent of those individuals were being cared for by relatives, who were struggling to live out their own lives while giving their charges a quality life. These caregivers were providing 10.9 million hours of care per year. Many of these people were in the unenviable position of trying to raise children as well. I felt very fortunate to not fall into that category.

I also learned that Lake County had almost nothing to offer caregivers in the area of assistance or resources. We were on our own, although I did get the name of a neurologist whom everyone seemed to like. I made an appointment with her for the month after Mom would be arriving. I was optimistic and hoped that she might say that Mollie didn't even have Alzheimer's disease.

CHAPTER 5

It Could Happen to You
Frank Sinatra – 1944

THE DAY OF Mollie's visit to the neurologist arrives, and after a stressful time of getting her ready, we are finally on our way.

I lay out her clothes and go to put my make-up on while she gets dressed. I choose a simple white long sleeved blouse and her black linen pants and low heeled black pumps. She looks very nice in this outfit. When I return, she has hung the clothes I laid out back onto hangers and has put her old sweat shirt and polyester pants back on. She just can't remember anything, so this time I stay and help her dress.

"Now, where are we going?" she asks for what seems like the fiftieth time during our twenty minute ride.

We're going to the doctor, Mom," I reply with as much composure as I can muster. I'm still miffed by the dressing fiasco.

"Am I sick?"

"No, you just have some problems with your memory," I say, thinking what a major understatement that is.

As we pull into the parking lot, I am surprised to see such a run-down building. The exterior is badly in need of a paint job and the landscaping has been terribly neglected. I should think a neurologist would have a better eye for aesthetics than this. I help Mom out of the car and we enter the building.

The waiting room is no better than the exterior of the building. We stand patiently at the receptionist desk while she busily whites out something on a chart and works very hard at giving us the impression she is producing another *War and Peace* and our presence is a horrible intrusion. She finally gives a disgusted sigh and asks, "What's the name?"

"Mollie Turner," I answer.

"Why, that's MY name," says Mom. This makes me chuckle.

"Have her fill out these papers," she says, handing me several pages.

As we find seats, I notice a heavyset man and woman, probably husband and wife, sitting across from us. The woman appears to be in her sixties and is very shabbily dressed. Her hair hangs in strings around her face and the front of her clothing is soiled. She is wearing an enormous pair of hoop earrings, which seem out of place with her other clothes.

Mom leans over to me and says in a not too quiet stage whisper, "Look at how fat that man is."

"Hush. It's not nice to talk like that." I feel my face flush, and I hope they didn't hear her.

The woman hits her husband on the leg and says in a loud voice, "Where is that nigger doctor, we don't have all day."

Her chubby husband looks at me apologetically and rolls his eyes. With great effort, he rises from the rather wobbly arm chair and laboriously walks over to me. The chair looks almost relieved as the fake leather covering noisily tries to reposition itself. The man's face is really quite attractive. There are no wrinkles and it has a pleasant sheen to it. His eyes are a beautiful magnetic blue with little flecks of green around the pupil.

"I think that fat man likes you," Mom whispers.

He hears her and appears to be amused. He rummages around in his pocket and finally pulls out what I think is a business card, which he hands to me. "You can get some of these from Dr. Jackson," he says. "They help smooth things out for us caregivers."

I look at the card. It simply says:

"My companion has Alzheimer's disease and may say or do things that seem inappropriate. Please excuse their behavior, they can't help it."

As if on cue, his wife hollers, "Freddie, get your fat ass back over here and stop trying to pick up that tramp."

Mollie bristles and retorts loudly, "We don't talk like that in New Jersey; and besides, that tramp is MY daughter-in-law... and your husband is really fat."

The woman doesn't respond and I quickly pat Mollie on the shoulder and hand her a magazine, hoping to defuse the situation. The chubby man seems to be amused and I find that mildly annoying. I am longing for that bottle of liquid paper that the receptionist was using to erase this scene. No, maybe to erase the life I am now living. This is the most embarrassing public moment I have had to deal with since Mollie has been with us.

As I find myself looking for a little respite from the dreary waiting room fiasco, "Tolstoy" the receptionist calls the man and his wife into the doctor's inner sanctum. I breathe a sigh of relief.

"Sherry," says Mom, "Did you see how fat that man was?" That seems to be all she remembers.

When it is our turn to go in, we are ushered into the examining room and left to wait. A poster on the wall shows a man with his healthy brain mapped out in blue and red; next to that is a second picture of him with large yellow areas, like abstract chrysanthemums, where the Alzheimer's disease has eradicated parts of his brain. It is a frightening pictorial, and I hope Mom doesn't see it.

"Now, where are we going?" she asks again.

When the doctor comes into the room, I hold my breath hoping Mollie won't say anything inappropriate. Dr. Jackson is a large, cheerful, black woman with a head full of dreadlocks and an infectious smile. "Well, how are we today?" she asks.

"I'm not sure about her, but I'm fine," Mollie replies gesturing toward me.

Dr. Jackson smiles.

"Before I examine you, we're going to do a little quiz to test your memory. First I'm going to give you five words. Here we go: Airplane, Applesauce, Giraffe, Rollercoaster and Football. Now, after I do a physical exam, I'm going to ask you to remember the words and repeat them to me. OK?"

She listens to Mollie's heart and takes her blood pressure (which is 110/65). I quietly wonder what my blood pressure is at that moment; much higher, I am sure.

Mollie is warming up to her. "Do you see these bruises on my arm?" she asks. Her skin is extremely thin and fragile and she almost always has bruises on her arms.

"My goodness, what in the world happened to you?" The doctor gently lifts her arm to examine it.

"SHE did that to me," Mom says, mischievously pointing her finger at me.

A chill runs down my spine as I envision myself on the evening news, being booked into the Lake County Jail for elder abuse.

I glance at Dr. Jackson. She is laughing and gives me a warm smile. I relax a bit and decide that I like her very much.

"Miss Mollie, you'd better be careful about saying things like that, you're liable to get your daughter-in-law in a lot of trouble. People around here take things like that very seriously, and I'm sure Sherry would never hurt you."

At that moment, she is dead wrong. I really feel like hitting Mollie for that comment.

"Now, let's see if you can remember the words I gave you." She says to Mollie. I wrack my brain: Giraffe, Applesauce, Football, and…

Mollie doesn't get any of them.

Dr. Jackson says they will need some definitive tests before she prescribes any medication. It seems that they can't positively determine if a patient has Alzheimer's or some other form of dementia, even after all the available tests; but based on her examination she is pretty sure she does. She is going to have a new genetic test done as well as an MRI. After the results, she assures me that they can put Mollie on medication that will slow the progression of the disease.

I am feeling good about this visit. I think we both liked the doctor and anything we can do to help keep Mollie from getting worse is what we all want. I intend to follow up vigorously.

When she lived in Tennessee, she went to a general practitioner who had put her on medication for Alzheimer's disease, but they had never had any confirmation that she actually had it. She had not reacted favorably to the prescription, and the girls didn't pursue it further. They weren't big believers in medication.

I view it a little differently than they did. First of all, Mollie is extremely healthy physically and her family genetics seem predisposed to her living a long life. I want the rest of it to be as good as it can be; not just for her, but as caregivers, for me and Bob as well. This is a step in the right direction.

CHAPTER 6

───── ❧ ─────

It's A Sin to Tell A Lie
The Ink Spots - 1936

As I HELP Mom back into the car, I suddenly feel an overwhelming fatigue. Is this the way my life will be from now on? I feel frightened that I will not be the caregiver that I had envisioned. I shake my head to rid myself of my unsettling thoughts.

"Let's stop and treat ourselves to a nice lunch at Olive Garden, how does that sound?" I say.

"I'd love to, but I don't have any money, and I think I've lost my purse." Mom replies.

I had learned that Mollie always did lose her purse, and as Mary suggested, I had stopped letting her carry it, but she still always thinks that she has lost it.

"I have your money in my purse and I'll let you treat."

"Is this the doctor's office?" Mollie says as we pull into Olive Garden.

"No, you've already been to the doctor, this is the restaurant."

"I've forgotten my purse." She squirms around in the seat as though trying to find it.

Mollie seems anxious and nervous as I help her out of the car and I try making small talk to relax her. As she takes her cane and we head for the door, I call her attention to the aromatic clump of rosemary in the flower bed, hoping to relax her. She has great appreciation for all growing things.

After we are seated and have our menus, I help her decide on a chicken and pasta dish and I order the soup and salad.

"I'm so glad you didn't order the fish for me. I can't stand fish," she says. "My father had a big old car when I was a girl. It was called a Grey. Times were hard then and to make a little extra money, Pops took the back seat out of that car. He would go down to the Delaware River and catch a bunch of fish. He'd fill that back seat area with ice, put all the mackerels on top, and drive around town selling them. That car always smelled like a mackerel and so did I. I've hated fish ever since."

This is a story that I had never heard. It is amazing how Mollie can remember such details from her childhood and almost nothing of her present life. I wonder to myself if she could be making it up.

Our food arrives and our server asks if we want grated cheese on top. He seems extremely nervous and I wonder why. He fidgets with the placement of our food, giving my order to Mollie and hers to me. He has also forgotten our beverages and is quite flustered when I call it to his attention.

"Have you been working here long?" I ask.

"This is my first day. I guess you can tell, huh?"

"You're doing a great job." I assure him. "As a matter of fact, I was going to ask you if you sell those cute little cheese graters."

"We do, and actually, we get points for each one we sell." He brightens a bit.

"Well, please add one to my bill and bring it when you give us the check."

"Sherry, do you have enough money for all this. I'm sure it will be expensive." Mollie asks. "I would like to treat, but I've lost my purse."

Even with the repetition about the nonexistent purse, we finish our meal pleasantly, and I feel myself relax after the stress of the day. Mom chats about some neighbor she had in New Jersey, and I pretty much tune her out.

When the server brings our check, he seems upset again.

"I am so sorry; we are out of the cheese graters." He is blushing and really rattled and I feel bad for him.

Just as I begin to reassure him, Mollie points her finger at him in a somewhat playful manner and in a loud voice says, "Liar, Liar, Pants on Fire."

I can't help myself, I burst out laughing.

"I'm sorry, she's just kidding you," I say as the waiter stands there, dumbfounded. I find myself wishing that I had asked the doctor for some of those cards that the man in the waiting room told me about. I make a mental note to do just that on the next visit.

I pay the check and we head for home. I can't wait to tell Bob this story.

As we ride home, I am deep in thought about our doctor's visit. Mom is quietly singing along with the radio. The doctor has told me that aside from her dementia, Mollie is remarkably healthy for her age. I am wondering how that might translate into the length of time she has left. Mollie is eighty-eight years old. I am sixty-two and Bob is soon to be sixty-four. If she lives another ten years, we will be well into our seventies, and it's not inconceivable that she could live even longer than that.

I'm ashamed to think this way, but this is not what I imagined my retirement years to be. We retired early from the printing business that we owned. I had pictured us traveling and taking vacations that we had never allowed ourselves during our working years. My mother was born in England and I always wanted to visit her homeland, and perhaps go to Ireland as well. Caring for Mollie will certainly not permit any of that activity. I want to be a good caregiver, but not at the expense of our leisure years. I hadn't thought about this scenario when I so enthusiastically welcomed Mollie into our lives.

I realized when we decided to move Mom into our home that the bulk of her care would fall to me. People have already said that they think Bob should be taking a more active part in the care of his mother. They just don't understand the dynamics of our relationship. We have been married for forty-four years and there have always been, by mutual agreement, defined roles for both of us. Caregiving, either for our children or aging parents, has always been in my realm. Household chores such as laundry or cooking and cleaning also fall to me, as does shopping and scheduling of health check-ups, and remembering birthdays and other family events.

Any type of maintenance on the house or cars including lawn up-keep is in Bob's area. In addition, he has always pursued woodworking and has custom-built many beautiful objects for our home. He completely remodeled our aging and dated kitchen; even building the cabinets from scratch. He built a huge farmhouse table for our dining room and a custom entertainment center that houses our television and sound system. He is an artisan at such projects and completely in his element.

This division of household responsibilities, although strange to younger people, has always worked well for us, even when we were both working outside our home and raising our family. This was how it was in Bob's family when he was growing up, and it just seems right to us both.

Besides, I have always loved his mother dearly; and although I am finding it more difficult than I anticipated, I am happy to do it. (I think.)

"Who's singing this song?" Mom breaks into my reverie.

"That's Perry Como. Remember how much you used to love his show on television?"

I think back to the first time I met Mollie. I was sixteen years old and had lived in Miami since my father died when I was seven. I met Bob through the window at Burger King, where I worked. We went to the movies a few times, but nothing more. However, Bob had a car, and since I had to walk to work, he always took me home after my shift. I didn't really want a steady boyfriend at that time, but I appreciated the ride. Bob, on the other hand, was quite smitten and wanted our relationship to go further.

One night on the ride home, he said, "I think it's time you met my family." He drove several blocks and pulled his ratty old '46 Ford in front of a modest ranch style home in a neatly kept subdivision. I was nervous as we walked up the sidewalk to the front door. I felt like he was out of my league. My house was in a neighborhood that had no sidewalks at all. My front yard was a sand pit, and his had beautifully manicured grass that was even edged next to the walkway. There were colorful flower beds and several palm trees next to the property line. In my yard, there was an old car propped up on cement blocks next to a sole pink flamingo, and there was no landscaping at all.

As we approached the front door, I heard his mother talking to his younger sister Mary, who was about twelve years old. "How am I supposed to know what the primary crop of South Africa is? Didn't you read your assignment?"

Wow, my mother never helped me with my homework. This was like *The Ozzie and Harriet Show.*

Bob and I went into the house. His dad was sitting in his chair reading the newspaper. His little sister, Kathy, who appeared to be about four years old, was lying on the floor on her stomach with her hands propping up her head, watching The Ed Sullivan Show.

I noticed that Mary did not look especially pleased to see me and I wondered if she was against her brother having a girlfriend. Mollie rushed forward to greet us. She was a pretty woman, with light brown, almost blonde hair. She wore a soft blue patterned house dress that buttoned down the front.

"Well, finally we get to meet Sherry, and you're just as pretty as Bobby said you were." She hugged me and I remember hoping that I didn't smell like the Whopper hamburgers I had been making all day.

I don't remember too much more about that evening, but I do know that Mollie won me over completely. We were destined to become best friends before I ever married her son.

As I steer the car into our driveway, I turn off my thoughts of the Mollie I knew. Bob comes over to the car and helps his mom out and into the house. She goes into her room, and I give Bob a little peck on the cheek. I am still basking in the warmth of my memories. It makes me sad to think that the Mollie of my memory is gone.

CHAPTER 7

⚬

Cheeseburger in Paradise
Jimmy Buffett - 1978

ONE OF THE most interesting aspects of Mollie's disease is that although she can remember nothing of her present life and not much of her adult life, she can remember, in startling detail, events that never happened. It is almost like she feels the need to compensate for her loss of real memories.

One morning as she is sitting at the table having her breakfast, she holds up a single Cheerio and says, "How do you suppose they make these cute little O's?"

I am standing at the kitchen sink rinsing dishes, "I don't know, Mom, but I imagine there is some kind of machine that punches them out. It would be interesting to see that. They could do a television show on it. Actually, I think they have a show called *How It's Made*. We should write and ask them to do one about Cheerios."

"I just think inventing things must be the most rewarding career in the world," she says as she takes another bite of Cheerios. "Did I ever tell you about meeting George Foreman, the Negro that invented that hamburger grill they sell on T.V.?" Her eyes sparkle at the memory of the encounter.

"Mom, are you sure you met "The" George Foreman? He was the heavyweight champion of the World. I think he was the boxer who fought Muhammad Ali in Africa. That would have been a long before he invented his grill. You never told me you met him." My curiosity is piqued and I find myself wondering if this could be true.

"Oh yes, it was that same George Foreman. He worked at DuPont with Uncle Frank and I was introduced to him at Cowtown when I went there with Emma and Frank. He had a booth set up and he was demonstrating and selling his grills right there. I think he had just started trying to market them."

As she talks, I remember that I visited Cowtown once when we were in New Jersey. It was a wonderful, old flea market near Pennsville where Bob's family had lived when he was a young boy. It had begun as a place for farmers to take their cattle to auction and then had expanded to include their crops. It wasn't long before it had evolved to a place where you could find pretty much anything that you wanted; from homemade jellies and pies, to fine china, to parts for your '52 Studebaker. It seemed almost plausible that someone might take an invention there to see how people received it. But still, I can't believe that's how the Foreman grill got its start; nor does it seem believable that George Foreman worked at DuPont with Uncle Frank.

"Why in the world would George Foreman be in Cowtown?" I ask.

"Well, he was there," she replies somewhat indignantly. "He worked with Uncle Frank at DuPont, and he had invented this hamburger grill. Why, his eyes just sparkled as he showed me how the grease would run right down into a little plastic tray. It's a lot healthier to drain the grease, you know."

"He was just a beautiful Negro. He had such pretty shiny skin, the color of milk chocolate candy, and a big smile with a mouthful of the whitest teeth I've ever seen. He was so tickled and proud of his new invention. I can see him right now." Her face is aglow.

"Why, I remember Frank, slapping him on the back and saying, 'Well George, I hope you make a million bucks with that thing, and don't you know that's just what he did. Why just about everyone I know has one. Sherry, I would gladly buy you one, if I had any money." Her story sounds very convincing, but I really think I would have heard it before if it were true.

She is holding a Cheerio up to the light again, rotating it in little circles. "How do you think they make these little O's?" she asks again.

"I'll be right back, Mom," I say as I pour her a fresh cup of coffee. "I just want to run out to the shop and ask Bob something."

Bob is sanding a shelf for the cabinet that he is building for our bedroom. He sees me and wipes his hands and says, "Do you need a break? Is Mom driving you crazy?"

"Not really, but listen to this. Have you ever heard about her meeting George Foreman?"

"Whoa, that's a new one."

I tell him her story, and he chuckles and says, "Well, that sounds pretty convincing, but I would have thought we'd have heard it before."

"I'm going to call Kathy in Tennessee and see what she knows about it. I'm really curious," I say.

As I tell the story to Kathy, she starts to laugh. "Oh my gosh, Mom drove Mary crazy with that story. Mary even looked Ole

43

George up on the internet, and he was born in the fifties some-where out in Texas. He never could have worked at DuPont, and certainly not with Uncle Frank. The age difference was too great. Mary gave Mom all that information, but she stubbornly insisted that "she knew what she knew" and that was all there was to it.

Mary went so far as to call Aunt Emma and got her to tell Mom that they had never met George Foreman, but Mom wouldn't give up. She even stopped using her George Foreman grill, be-cause every time Mom saw it, she would launch into the whole story again. I'll say one thing; the story was always consistent, right down to poor old George's shiny skin and white teeth. I'm surprised this is the first time you've heard it."

"Wow," I say to Bob after we hang up. "That is really weird. Why in the world would she make up a story like that and about George Foreman, no less? Have you noticed that she seems to have a preoccupation with black people?"

"I guess she does, but remember things were a lot different when she grew up. I guess that's to be expected."

When I walk back into the house, Mom is still sitting in the kitch-en working on her crossword puzzle. She has written the date, Dec. 16, 1917 in the margin several times.

"Sherry, what is today's date?" she asks.

"It's right at the top of the paper." I reply.

"Oh, yes June 10, 2005." She subtracts the numbers and says, "Well, that would make me eighty-eight years old, wouldn't it? How in the world did I get so old?"

Mollie has always talked about her age and she can always remember her birth date. We do this little ritual almost every morning. She seems to have forgotten her George Foreman story, thank goodness.

"I think I'll make hamburgers for dinner tonight. Does that sound alright with you?"

"That sounds great!" she replies, "Are you going to fix them on a George Foreman grill? Did I ever tell you how I met him one time at Cowtown? He had just invented that grill..."

CHAPTER 8

———— ❡ ————

If I Only Had A Brain
Ray Bolger "The Scarecrow" - 1939

THE DAY OF Mollie's MRI appointment arrives. Dr. Jackson has scheduled it because the results of the genetic test were inconclusive for Alzheimer's, and the doctor feels that this test will give us a more definitive diagnosis, one way or the other.

Bob is trying his best to be involved in his mother's care and has offered to take her, but I want to be the one to follow through on this. He's fine with that explanation, even a little relieved, I think.

It has already been a trying morning, and I am second-guessing my refusal of Bob's offer. I have laid out her clothes twice; and twice she has hung them neatly back on the hangers and redressed in her "around the house garb." I inhale deeply, trying to squelch my aggravation as I help her dress. When will I learn that I need to stay and monitor her dressing?

Bob has pulled the car right up next to our front door and he is gently moving her in that direction. "Oh Bobby, look at your beautiful new car," she says as he helps her into the seat and buckles her seatbelt.

"No Mom, it's the same old car."

"Bobby, I think you have my jock strap too tight." She tugs on the seatbelt.

He laughs and replies, "You might want to remember that it's called a seatbelt. People will look at you funny if you call it that."

He looks at me and rolls his eyes. I am laughing too, and it helps to break the tension of getting her ready and into the car.

We are finally on our way and she asks me for the umpteenth time, "Now, where are we going?"

"We're going to get a test on your brain, and it won't hurt a bit. I'll be right in the room with you. They want to try to find out exactly what medicine they can give you to help you remember things better." I try to sound reassuring.

She immediately starts singing the Scarecrow's song from "The Wizard of Oz."

I could while away the hours conferring with the flowers,
Consulting with the rain
And my head I'd be a scratchin'
While my thoughts are busy hatchin'
If I only had a brain

I think this is pretty cute, but my response is a bit testy. "You definitely have a brain, or you wouldn't be able to remember the lyrics to every song you've ever heard."

"Good Sherry" is giving me a dirty look for being so crabby. "Anyway, if I can find this place, they're going to check you out."

Mollie suddenly looks frightened. "Sherry, what if they don't find anything up there. You know how bad my memory is. What will happen to me if I don't pass the test? What if something really bad is wrong with me?" She sounds genuinely concerned.

I feel sorry for her and answer gently, "Nothing will happen to you. Your life won't change one iota if they find something wrong. You'll still live with Bob and me, just like you do now. The reason for the test is to make sure that you're on the proper medication to help you live the best life possible."

As I say this, I think about some of the things I have learned about Alzheimer's disease: the rapid memory decline, the possible personality changes, the gradual deterioration of one's bodily functions, until some people even lose the ability to swallow their food. I feel guilty down-playing the ramifications such a diagnosis might entail, but I certainly don't want to tell her all this.

Mollie seems to have lost her interest and concern because she now remarks, "Every time we drive down this street, I see that same fat man in those dirty old overalls crossing at this very same light. Where do you think he's going?"

"Really?" I respond, knowing full well that she has never been on this road in her life. This is another strange aspect of her condition: she always comments that she has seen the same person, same car, same house, same church … whatever. I wonder if this is a subconscious effort on her part to try to camouflage her memory loss.

We arrive at the radiology center, and after the usual forms and a short wait, a young man with a British accent guides us into a room containing a huge, whale-like contraption that I assume is the MRI machine. I am surprised that this gentleman is the technician because of his youth, but he seems quite professional as he helps Mollie onto the table in front of the machine. He secures her head into a mold, which is designed to keep her immobile. He then places a wedge under her knees to raise her legs a bit and make her more comfortable.

Mollie lies quietly on the table and she looks terrified. Her eyes are scrunched tightly closed, and her hands are clasped across the front of her body. I feel sorry for her and I walk over and take one of her hands. She shakes uncontrollably.

"Well, Lovey," he gushes. "That should do it. Just lie very still and breathe in and out when I tell you to. It's a noisy bugger, but it won't hurt you a bit. Your daughter and I will be behind that wall watching you."

"Is there any way I can sit closer to her? I'm afraid she'll try to get up," I say.

"Alright then, as long as you have no metal on, I'll get a chair, and you can sit right here next to her."

"What are you going to do to me?" she asks in a childish manner.

"I'm going to take some photos of your brain," he replies.

Mom immediately bursts into the, *"If I only had a brain"* song.

The technician laughs and replies, "Not to worry, Lovey. I'm sure you have a very comely brain." His comment seems to reassure her, and I decide that this guy is pretty cool.

The entire time the test is going on, with the machine sounding as though it is mixing concrete, Mollie does exactly what she is told. Each time the whale swallows her up, emitting thumps and groans, she just lies there, perfectly still and totally obedient.

I keep hollering reassurances to her, telling her the test is almost over and that she's doing great, but she doesn't really seem to need them. I feel a surge of pride. I remember feeling this way when my daughter Jennifer was only six and she broke her leg. She held my hand tightly and didn't cry one little bit while the doctor set her leg.   I bragged about her every chance I got.

When the test is completed, the technician helps her up and explains that the neurologist will call us with the results.

"Did you see my brain?" asks Mollie.

"That I did, Lovey, and a more beautiful brain I've never seen."

She reaches over and takes his hand, raising it to her lips and gently kissing it. It's a sweet moment.

As I help Mollie get her cane situated so we can leave, the technician pats me on the shoulder as though he feels I am doing a good job. I feel undeserving and I am suddenly overcome with guilt.

The neurologist calls several days later and tells us that although a firm diagnosis of Alzheimer's disease is almost impossible in a living person, all of the signs from both the MRI and the genetic testing, coupled with the fact that her older sister died from the disease, make it pretty certain that Mollie has Alzheimer's.

She prescribes two medications that taken together are the standard treatment at the time. There is no cure, but these are thought to slow its progression. We had hoped the news would be better, but we resolve to do our best for Mollie and stay on top of any promising research. I try to pin Bob down as to what we will do if her capacity diminishes rapidly.

"We'll take this journey one step at a time. Circumstances will tell us what to do," he says.

This answer really doesn't satisfy me, but I don't know what would.

CHAPTER 9

❧

C'est Si Bon
Eartha Kitt - 1953

AT THE BEGINNING of this journey, Bob and I had determined that we would find things to do that would include his mother. We live close to a large retirement community. Many of its amenities are for residents only, but some are open to the public. One such venue is a non-denominational church, which frequently has free concerts.

Bob is involved in a project, and I know he won't want to go with us, so one afternoon I get Mom all dressed, and we go there to see a Big Band concert. This was the music that she grew up with, and I am not disappointed in the level of appreciation that she has. She sings along robustly with almost every song they play. When they play their finale, which is *"Little Brown Jug,"* she beams with happiness. She begs me to let her go up on the stage to thank them personally. I dissuade her from that, but I am basking in good feelings for having thought to do this. I know without a doubt that, in spite of "Evil Sherry," I am a totally awesome caregiver.

As we make our way out to the public square, she notices some people line-dancing in front of the entertainment pavilion.

"Oh Sherry, could we go over there and watch those old people dance?" she asks. Mollie always thinks people are older than she is, even when they are obviously younger. It's funny.

"I think that's a great idea. We can sit and have a cold drink and enjoy some more music." My idea of a cold drink at six o'clock in the evening involves a man named Mr. Bacardi and a wedge of lime, and that is a definite option here.

We find two seats near the dance floor, and I get her settled and head to the "Libation Station." When I return with a ginger ale for her and my beverage of choice, I see that she is chatting amiably with an older gentleman, who appears to be a bit younger than she. He is wearing the unofficial uniform for village gentlemen: plaid Bermuda shorts, a print Polo shirt, and sneakers with knee-high socks. His rather long gray hair has been artfully combed across the top of a quite shiny bald area.

As I get closer, I realize that she is speaking a little of her high school French to the gentleman. "Parlez-vous Français?"

He looks a little helpless when he sees me and says, "She told me she lived in New Jersey and when I told her I was from Paris, Ohio, she started speaking French." Addressing Mollie, he says, "Well, it was nice talking to you." He bustles away in the direction of the bar.

"Au revoir, Monsieur," Mollie shouts after him.

This is hilarious. I laugh and give Mollie a little wink. "You've still got it, girl." I wonder if he was hitting on her. She doesn't look that much older than he appears to be. This community has a bit of a reputation for being a place for older folks to find romance and maybe that's what he was looking for. Mollie is certainly an attractive woman for her age.

We sit and watch the line dancers strut their stuff. It's a mild day in early May, and I think how nice it is to sit outdoors and just relax. I am still feeling upbeat about Mollie's enjoyment of the concert, and my image of myself as a good caregiver.

"Wasn't that concert great? I think that band played some of those old songs every bit as good as the recordings I've heard of Glenn Miller," I say.

"Oh, I would love to have seen that," she replies. "Can I go with you next time?"

I feel as though I have been punched in the stomach. Does she really have no recollection of something she appeared to enjoy so thoroughly and so recently?

"Mom," I hear a whiny, scolding sound to my voice. "We just came from that concert. It was right over in that church. We were just there." I point to the building.

She looks startled at my tone and a bit confused as well. "I think I would remember if I went to a concert."

"Yeah, I would think so too." I drain the contents of my glass and abruptly rise. "I'm going to get another drink, just stay here until I get back." I stride across the pavilion, all warm, fuzzy thoughts banished and "Evil Sherry" taking the reins gleefully.

As I start to walk back with my drink, I see three of my old friends, strolling across the patio. They are laughing, and I feel a stab of jealousy. These girls and I have been pretty tight for the last few years. We did a lot of girl things together: movie dates, spa dates, a ski trip. Since Mollie has come, I haven't been included, and I miss it … and, fairly or not, I blame her.

I duck behind a palm tree, hoping they won't see me. I don't feel like acting friendly at the moment. Besides, if I start explaining about the concert and Mollie, I'm afraid they'll think I'm a whiner. They keep walking down the sidewalk, away from the pavilion and I see them enter a restaurant.

I return to where I left Mollie. "Well, I wondered where you went," she sounds reproachful. I toss my untouched drink in the trash basket and help her to her feet. "Let's head for home. Bobby will be wondering where we are."

We head for the car without speaking. I feel like all I want is a good cry.

Later that evening after I have fixed Mollie's dinner and gotten her settled in to watch her television programs, I go out to Bob's shop. It has become a ritual that I really look forward to. As usual, everything about his work area is neat and tidy. The shelves are filled with bins, which are all labeled on the front with their contents. He is just finishing sweeping up the sawdust when I walk in the side door.

"Hi, how's it going? I'm glad you didn't go with us to the concert. It was pretty depressing."

"You're kidding me. I can't believe she didn't enjoy it. She has such an appreciation for music."

"Oh, she enjoyed the concert alright. As a matter of fact, she loved it. She sang along at the top of her voice, almost to the point that I was embarrassed, but ten minutes after it was over, she had no recollection of it at all."

I walk to his refrigerator and get myself a glass of wine. "I'm not sure I'm going to be able to do this." I say as I slump onto the stool next to his workbench and suddenly the pent-up tears of the day let loose.

Bob puts down the broom and comes up behind me. He puts his hand on my shoulder. "Honey, you're trying too hard. You can't change what's happened to Mom. You can't make her better. I can't make her better. We just have to deal in the best way we know how. You say she loved the concert. You say she enjoyed the moment. That's enough. We want her time with us… her last years, to be pleasant; and you are doing all that you can to achieve that. You can't do anything more." He comes around and pulls me close.

"I just didn't think it would be so hard," I blubber into his shoulder. He smells like varnish, and I inhale deeply. It's a manly smell that I have grown to love.

"This isn't what I expected." I pull away and confront him face to face.

"What about us? Bob, it's an awful thing to say or even think; but physically, your mother is probably healthier than we are. She'll probably outlive both of us. This isn't what I thought our retirement would be. I know you're perfectly content to putter around on your projects, but I need more. I don't even see my friends anymore. I don't go anywhere, and I don't do anything fun." I am really getting this pity party cranked.

"Sherry, this isn't getting us anywhere. We talked about this, and we both agreed that it would be hard and that it would mostly fall on you. I keep trying to take over some of your self-perceived responsibilities. You won't let me. I don't know if it's a martyr thing or what, but just tell me what I can do to make it easier."

I suddenly feel deflated. I don't know the answer. He's right. I do want to be the hero, the martyr, the one who sacrifices all … but I guess I really don't, do I?

I get up, shake my head, and slosh back the rest of wine. "I don't know what I want. Dinner will be ready in about an hour. I'll come back out in a little while. Maybe I'll get it figured out."

As I walk across the yard, watching the full moon reflecting on the lake, I wonder, would I feel this way if it was <u>my</u> mother?

CHAPTER 10

The Way We Were
Barbra Streisand - 1973

I HAVE GIVEN a lot of thought to my discussion with Bob the other night. I realize that he was right on many counts; but I also realize that our life together as husband and wife has undergone a change. Our episodes of intimacy have diminished. It is hard to say how much of that can be attributed to his mother's presence and how much is just natural aging on our part. I also realize that I have not exactly been warm and fuzzy lately; maybe that's a factor. I decide that I need to make more of an effort.

One of the things that Bob and I had enjoyed was the spontaneity of our pre-Mollie life. Sometimes, we would both dress up a little, and have a little romantic dinner on the patio. After the number of years that we have been married, it is kind of hard to look sexy to one another, but we gave it the old college try. I decide one evening to try to rekindle that feeling. I fix Mom's dinner early and get her settled in front of the television.

"When are you and Bobby going to eat?" she asks.

"We're gonna cook a couple of steaks and eat on the patio. You don't like steak, so that's why I fed you early." I really want our little date to turn out well and I am wishing she would just go to bed.

"Why are you all dressed up?" she asks. "Are we going out?"

"No Mom, I just decided to try and look pretty for my husband. We're having a little dinner date on the patio."

"Oh how nice, what are we having for dinner?" she asks.

"Bob and I are having steak. You already had chicken and mashed potatoes, remember?"

Bob comes out from his shower, whistling and looking pretty darn good. He brings a plate of cookies and some coffee to his mother and she seems pleased.

"Enjoy your dessert," he says. "Sherry and I are going to eat out on the patio."

While he fires up the grill, I put some of our favorite CDs on the stereo. I throw together his favorite salad and join him outside, leaving the side door open so we can hear the music. I have brought out two of our fancy wine glasses and I fill one for each of us. He pulls me into an embrace as I hand him his wine.

"Umm, you smell good enough to eat." He nuzzles my neck. "Why don't we do this more often?" I give him a long hug and pull him close to me. The old familiar feelings flood over me.

The evening is picture-perfect. A full moon is just rising over the lake, its glow reflecting like a million little diamonds. The Spanish moss hanging from the oak boughs is gently swaying in the slight breeze, creating an almost mystical feeling. The crickets and frogs are singing their own love songs.

I watch my husband's back as he tends the grill. He is still such a good-looking man and my feelings for him swell with the rising crescendo of Linda Ronstadt's rendition of *"What's New."*

Suddenly, the side door slams, and Mom totters out with her cane. "Why are you both outside? Isn't it time for dinner?"

"We're going to eat some steaks out here, Mom. You already had a nice dinner, remember?" My voice is more peevish than I wish. *Oh, please don't let her ruin this night for us. Why can't she just go to bed? This is so unfair. What about me and my life?*

I give Bob "the look" and he goes over and walks her back in the house, while she chatters on about how much he would enjoy the T.V. program she is watching.

"Why don't you just sit in this chair and watch it with me?" she says. I hear him say something about our not having eaten yet, but I am so busy feeling slighted that I tune it out.

He stays in with her for a while, so I finish cooking the steaks and plate them up with the salad I prepared. I pour more wine and sit by myself gazing at the lake. The magic has gone and when he comes back out, we eat our food in relative silence.

"You realize that she didn't do that on purpose, don't you?" he says.

I'm furious that he is making excuses for her. *Don't my feelings count at all?*

I should confront him, but I nod my head in affirmation; the lump in my throat keeping me from speaking. I sneak a look at him as he cuts his steak and eats his salad. His jaw is set in the familiar way that shows his annoyance. I'm hoping it's not all directed at me, that would seem quite unfair; but he has always expected me to take the high road. Every time I relate a story to him about someone who has slighted me in some way, he almost always makes me feel as though I somehow deserved it. I doubt that has changed. He has stopped trying to make conversation, and I am not feeling conciliatory either, so we finish eating in strained silence.

I turn off the music and clear the table. While I do the dishes, Bob goes out to his workshop. I know he's expecting me to join him as I usually do in the evening; but I change into my nightgown and go to bed by myself. I leave Mollie watching television. She can figure out how to get to bed on her own.

The next morning when I wake up, Bob has already risen. I get dressed and go out to the living room where he is reading the paper.

"Good morning," he says. "What happened to you last night, I thought after that nice dinner, you'd come out for a nightcap."

I'm furious at him for minimizing the outcome of the evening. He's acting like nothing happened. "I was tired so I just went to bed. Did you help Mom get settled?" my tone is quite cold.

"No, when I came in, the television was blaring, but her door was closed, so I didn't bother her."

"Well, I better go check on her. She probably sat up all night."

I quietly open Mom's door and tiptoe in. She's sound asleep with her hands clasped together as if in prayer. She's wearing the nightgown with little rosebuds on it that she got last Mother's Day from Kathy. Her hair is haloed around her head on the pillow. She is the picture of innocence and I feel a stab of guilt.

As I quietly close the door, I realize that my mutiny of the previous evening seems to have had little effect on anyone except me. I also realize that I am mildly annoyed that they seem to have managed quite well without me.

CHAPTER 11

❧

What'll I Do
Judy Garland - 1964

I AM STILL feeling guilty and out-of-sorts this afternoon, and I decide I will give Mollie my full attention. She is sitting in her chair in the family room with the wicker basket of her photographs on her lap. I am so grateful that the girls thought to send these. This is Mollie's favorite pastime, the pictures span her entire lifetime. I am sitting on the floor in front of her trying to pay attention as she points out pictures of people and places from her past. She seems to recognize the older photographs much better than the more recent ones.

She holds up a black and white, eight by ten photograph of a young woman seated on a stool at an austere industrial-looking table. I recognize it immediately as a young Mollie.

"Why this is a picture of me when I worked at DuPont in the rubber lab. I was really lucky to get that job when Bob was sent to France. They had given him a deferral until after Bobby was born, but when the baby was three months old, they shipped his daddy overseas.

"I had been hired right out of high school into a secretarial position, but when many of the men went into the service their

63

jobs had to be filled by women. Do you remember hearing about "Rosie, the riveter?" Well, I think that campaign is why I was offered Robert Humphrey's job as a rubber batch control checker. I loved that job."

I get up from the floor and settle myself in the other recliner. I love to hear these stories from her past, and it always amazes me that in light of her memory problems, she can remember them in such vivid detail.

She goes on, "My mother and I were still estranged, and I was on my own with a baby boy. On my salary alone, I couldn't afford the house that Bob and I had rented, and so I found a small apartment in a building that housed three other families. I was on the second floor. The apartment was located several blocks from the ferry boat that took me across the river to my job at DuPont. I sat at a large table on a stool and put various batches of rubber through a lot of tests. I measured their strength and flexibility and recorded all of my figures carefully into a log. This was an important job and I took it very seriously."

She pauses for a moment to point out a chickadee at the bird feeder outside the window, but I want her to go back to her story, so I don't say anything to distract her.

"Every morning, I got up at five o'clock. I washed Bobby's diapers and hung them on a line that I had strung over the top of the radiator in the little kitchen. In the summer, I had been able to hang them in the basement of the building, but now that it was winter that didn't work. In early November, I went down the stairs to retrieve the diapers and they had been frozen solid. As I carried them up the stairs, they reminded me of the tablets of stone that Moses had inscribed the Ten Commandments on." She chuckles and takes a sip of her coffee.

I am enjoying hearing this story in more detail than I have heard it before. I am amazed at her ability to remember so much of what happened more than sixty years ago. She continues from right where she left off, which surprises me, as continuity is something she now struggles with.

"Things were much harder in those days. Once I finished washing the clothes in the kitchen sink, I would make Bobby's Pablum and formula. I had to hurry because once he woke up and started to cry, I had to keep him quiet by sticking a bottle in his mouth. The moment he started crying, mean old Mrs. Braun, the German lady who lived downstairs, would bang on her ceiling with a broom. I think she was mad because we were fighting the Germans. Anyway, I loved that little baby boy dearly, but he had the most annoying cry that anyone had ever heard. My sister-in-law, Emma, said he sounded just like a donkey braying. That really hurt my feelings, but I had to admit it was pretty awful.

"Once I finished all that, if I had time, I would make myself a cup of tea. We didn't have tea bags in those days and I had to pour the boiling water over leaves in the teapot and then strain the tea into a cup. Oh, I longed for a cup of coffee, but I usually had used all my ration cards and tea would have to do. I could smell the coffee brewing in Elmer and Tilly's apartment across the hall, but I tried not to think about it.

"After that, I had to get Bobby into his snowsuit. By that time the bells were ringing at St. Agatha's Catholic Church, and I had to hurry. (I wrote a little poem about this and sent it to Bob. I called it *The Bells of St. Aggie's*.) I struggled down the stairs with Bobby and walked six blocks to the nursery. He always cried when I dropped him off, and it broke my heart. I usually arrived at the ferry dock still in tears; but once I got on the ferry, I just tried to think about my job. The trip was torturous in the winter and everyone was chilled to the bone by the time we got to the plant."

She takes another sip of coffee and says, "You won't believe the rest of this story, it's like the crooked things that go on today. I can't believe that I was a part of it."

"Go on Mom," I urge as I push back the recliner and get comfortable. I am totally enthralled.

"Well, I had been at my job for several months and I was pretty good at it. It was up to me to check the different batches of rubber and make sure they were up to snuff."

"I guess they would call that quality control today," I interject.

She nods and continues, "On this particular morning, I took a glob of rubber out of the stainless steel tray and placed it on the table in front of me. I weighed the rubber and recorded the batch number and weight in my log. I then stretched it out to affix it to a clamp on each side of my machine. When I turned on the machine, it began to stretch the rubber, much like the taffy-pulling machines that they have on the boardwalk in Atlantic City. As the rubber slowly pulled out and stretched, it acquired a shiny finish. This particular piece just didn't look right to me. I checked all my adjustments and found that everything was set up properly but for some reason this piece was stretching unevenly. When the cycle finished, I measured the thickness with my micrometer and found that it was too thin in some areas and much too thick in others. I recorded all the measurements, and with my heart pounding, I approached Mr. Finley's desk.

"Mr. Finley was my supervisor, and he made me nervous. He looked like a character out of a Dickens novel. He was a scrawny man with rheumy, colorless eyes that watered all the time. He didn't like working with a roomful of women and made no secret of the fact that he thought we were not smart enough for this important kind of work." She giggled and added, "He also had the biggest Adam's apple tht I have ever seen, and I found it hard to look at him."

'Mr. Finley, I have a big problem,' I said softly.

'What might that be, cramps or some other female problem?' He sniffed loudly as he peered at me over the top of his spectacles.

"'No, Mr. Finley. There's a problem with one of the batches of rubber. The numbers are not right, and the rubber has a strange texture and finish. It's a batch from the Deepwater #9 Plant. Could you come take a look at it?'

"Mr. Finley swallowed several times, causing his enormous Adam's apple to bob alarmingly up and down in this throat. 'You've undoubtedly made some kind of mistake. We haven't had a bad batch of rubber in over 181 days.'

"He came over to my table and checked my log book. He then reviewed the manner in which I had secured the rubber. He began making little harrumphing sounds deep in his throat. 'This is highly unusual, I need to get Mr. Cicero to come and take a look at what you have done.' He left the lab quickly.

"Mr. Cicero was a pompous Italian man, who had a reputation about town as a ladies' man. He was very haughty and extremely vain about his appearance; particularly his moustache, which he paid to have groomed weekly at the barber shop. All of the townspeople felt sorry for his long-suffering wife, Angela. She had borne his six children, and he treated her as if she were his servant. It was obvious that whatever money he had, he shared sparingly with his family.

"'Oh Gawd,' shouted my friend, Connie Grundy from across the room. 'Cicero is going to fry you. I think his bonus depends on never having a bad batch of rubber. I'm glad it was your tray and not mine.'

"'Thanks a lot, Connie.' My heart was pounding loudly in my ears and I was scared to death. Everybody hated Mr. Cicero, and we avoided encounters with him at all costs … and now I was about to have one.

"Mr. Finley and Mr. Cicero entered the room with purpose. Finley was all atwitter and it seemed obvious that he didn't like Mr. Cicero very much either. Mr. Cicero swaggered over to my table and said in a booming voice for all to hear. 'Well young lady, I hear you've made some kind of mistake. Are you aware that Robert Humphrey worked at this very table for eight years and never once did he make a mistake in his calibrations?'

Yes, I thought angrily, and he was paid three times what you pay me and his penmanship was so bad that no one can even read his log entries to this day.

"With great flourish Mr. Cicero took another blob of rubber from the tray. I watched as he tried twice to affix it to the stationary arm of the stretcher. When he finally secured it, he turned the machine on and the rubber began to stretch and pull out. Just as it reached its maximum length, it snapped apart with a loud noise and a piece of it landed squarely in his carefully groomed moustache. I heard a stifled gasp from the other girls in the room. Mr. Cicero removed the gooey mess from his moustache, and said loudly and with great authority, 'There, it's just as I thought, you didn't read your micrometer correctly.'

"He turned and stalked out of the room as if he had completely remedied the problem. Mr. Finley went back to his desk at the front of the room, and that was that."

Mollie pauses a moment and stares off into space as she re-lives that moment in her mind. I am anxious for her to continue. "Oh my gosh, what did you do then?" I ask.

"I was furious, but what could I do? Later in the day as I was rushing to catch the ferry, Connie caught up with me.

"'Mollie, what are you gonna do? Cicero will never admit that there was a bad batch of rubber. What are you gonna do?'

"'I don't know, Connie. The easy thing would be to just let it go, but I keep thinking about our guys … my Bob, driving a jeep in France with inferior tires on it. What would you do?'

"'Jeez, I don't know, Mollie. If you pursue it, you'll probably get canned; and you've got little Bobby to think about, what then?'

"'I don't know what to do.' I said again.

"I barely slept that night. I could not get the events of the day out of my mind. The next day when I went to my table in the lab, I noticed that my log book was not in its usual place. When I opened it, I saw that all of my entries from the previous day were gone. The entire page had been neatly cut out of the book. I felt my face flush and I could hardly breathe. Clutching my log book, I went to Mr. Finley's desk. He saw me coming and his Adam's apple started bobbing like a cork with a fish on the line.

"'Mollie, um … Mrs. Turner,' he was almost whispering, 'please, just let it go.'

"I didn't say a word. I just walked to the door with my log book in hand.

"'Mrs. Turner, come back here immediately.' I ignored him and kept walking. I noticed that all the women were watching me and when I caught a glimpse of Connie, she was white as a ghost. I walked up the stairs to the executive floor and went straight to

Mr. Buckingham's office. I knocked on his door just as his secretary was trying to head me off.

"'Come in,' he said in a booming voice, and in I went.

"Mr. Buckingham was a gentle giant. He had been recalled from retirement to oversee the plant during the war effort. Everyone knew his track record, and he was widely respected and admired. I especially appreciated that he knew the names of all the women who were filling in for the men and he treated us with great respect. He made us feel that we were making our own contribution to our country and the war effort.

"'Mollie Turner, what can I do for you?'

It was hard, but I explained the events of the previous day. I showed him my altered log book and I wrote down the calibrations exactly as I remembered them from the missing page. I told him how much I needed my job but that I couldn't live with the fact that we might be supplying inferior rubber to our troops and what the ramifications might be. I began to cry but I was able to relate the story just as it occurred.

"Mr. Buckingham put his arm around my shoulder in a fatherly fashion. He told me that he admired me for having the courage to tell him this. He told me to take the rest of the day off and go home and play with little Bobby. His last words to me were, 'Mollie, I don't want you to worry. You have done the right thing.'

"The next day when I got to the rubber lab, Mr. Davis was seated at Mr. Finley's desk. At lunch, I found out from Connie that Mr. Finley and Mr. Cicero had been fired. All of the women that I worked with treated me like I was a hero."

She looks up and smiles at me as she finishes her story. I am astounded at her total recall of this event.

"That is an incredible story. How in the world can you re-member every detail with such clarity?"

"It's like a movie running inside my head. I can see all those people like it was yesterday. I can see my husband, Bob, too; but I know he grew old and I can only picture him when he was young. Do you think there is something wrong with my brain?" she says.

She is so earnest as she says this. I am taken aback. I don't know how to answer.

"None of us remembers everything," I stammer.

I help her gather up her pictures and put them back in the basket.

"Why don't you and I take a walk down to the mailbox? We both could use the exercise," I say.

I am quiet as we walk down the lane. Mollie's bravery in the story she just told has filled me with admiration for her. She de-serves so much more kindness than I give her and I silently vow to have more patience.

She notices everything as we walk along. She stops and bends over to pull a weed out of the grass. She stares up into the trees trying to locate the little wren that is loudly proclaim-ing his presence. She swishes an errant clump of moss with her cane. It takes us forever to reach the mailbox, and I feel my patience evaporate with every step.

Maybe there is something wrong with my brain, I think.

CHAPTER 12

—∾—

Skylark
Anita O'Day - 1941

As THE MONTHS pass, I realize that everyone else seems to be adjusting to their new roles fairly well. Mom has stopped talking about going home and now actually thinks that she owns our house and that we are living with her. This might be because Mary lived with her and Dad in Tennessee, although she rarely mentions Mary anymore. She is always saying things like, "Where in the world did I get the money to buy this nice house? I wish my mother could see it, she would be so proud."

Bob seems very satisfied just puttering around the shop on his projects. He has been working on building the new cabinets for our kitchen remodeling, which is a huge time consuming job. He finds great satisfaction in the thought that his mother is being well cared for in her declining years, and he is quick to give me the credit.

I am the only malcontent in the equation. I just can't seem to accept that Mollie is no longer the person she was before her disease. I know that she can't follow through on any task; or for that matter even remember that there was a task; and yet I keep giving her things to do and making her feel bad when she can't do them. For instance, I will take her with me into the yard to weed a flower bed and she will start pulling weeds like crazy, but the next time I look at her, she's pulling out the flowers and leaving the weeds. Why can't I accept her disabilities and work with them? I wonder if I somehow expect her to miraculously revert to the old Mollie of my memory. I read about people being in the state of denial on many issues, and wonder if that is my problem. Maybe I'm the one that needs treatment.

On this beautiful spring day, Mollie has risen earlier than usual. She is out on the screened porch. The sun is high in the sky, and the contrast of the green grass and clear water of the lake against its radiant blueness is stunning. The birds perched in the oaks are competing with each other to see whose song is livelier. The squirrels are chasing each other around the base of the trees. Their antics are so amusing to watch. It is going to be a warm day, and the shaded porch with its red brick patio and white wicker chairs with contrasting plaid cushions seems like a little retreat inviting us to just sit and enjoy the view.

I notice that Mollie is dusting the ledges along the screening with a well-worn, wadded-up tissue.

"Mom, that's a great idea, but let me give you something that will work." I hand her a Swiffer dusting wand. "The porch really needs a good dusting and it would help me a lot if you would do it."

"Oh, I'd love to help you, and that is just the cutest little duster." She takes it from my hand and starts waving it around as though she is conducting an orchestra. She then begins dusting like mad. I feel very gratified and go back into the house. This is something she can do that will make her feel useful. Besides, I absolutely hate to dust.

The next time I look out the window, she is outside of the screening on the patio. She is vigorously dusting the azalea hedges for all she is worth. She is still conducting her symphony, accenting each movement with emphasis.

"Mom, what are you doing?"

She jumps at the tone of my voice and I can feel the tug of war begin within me.

"Give the poor old lady a break. You know she can't help it. What's the matter with you?" says "Good Sherry".

"I'm the one that needs the break, she's always trying to ag-gravate me," counters "Evil Sherry".

"Mom, you don't need to dust the plants. People don't dust plants. You're supposed to be dusting the woodwork on the porch. That would be nice. That would actually help me. Dusting the azaleas is not at all helpful. Why can't you see that?" "Evil Sherry" is clearly in charge and quite sarcastic.

"Good Sherry" tries valiantly, *"The only reason you're so up-set is because you hate to dust. Aren't you ashamed of yourself?"*

As I am grappling with these feelings and trying to quell my aggravation, I see Mollie pick something out of the azalea bush-es and hold it high for me to see. It's a brilliantly colored Blue Jay feather, quite large and almost iridescent in the sunlight.

"Sherry, would you just look at this beautiful blue feather." Her wrinkled face is aglow with a childlike appreciation for such a simple pleasure. She clasps it to her breast as though it is a pre-cious treasure presented to her by God himself. She then bursts into a perfect Ella Fitzgerald rendition of *Skylark*.

"Good Sherry" smiles broadly and "Evil Sherry" slinks under a rock somewhere.

The porch, however, remains undusted.

CHAPTER 13

—— ⚯ ——

I've Got You Under My Skin
Frank Sinatra - 1946

MOLLIE HAS BEEN with us now for about six months, and I am learning that it isn't the big things about her condition, but the little things that drive me crazy. She is mildly incontinent and as a result, she wears pads to help keep her dry. This embarrasses her, and she pretty much takes care of them herself. The problem is that when she has soiled one, she does not put it in her garbage pail. Instead, she hides it. Sometimes, I find it neatly wrapped in toilet paper in the shower stall, but sometimes it's in a dresser drawer or in her closet. I always keep a close count, and I'm frequently going on scavenger hunts to make the count tally. Whenever I complain to her, she insists that she would never do something like that and I am surely mistaken.

Hiding things seems to be a common condition of dementia. Whenever Mollie takes off her watch, she puts it in a different place. Sometimes, it's wrapped in a sweater or scarf in her drawer. Once she hid it in her shoe. On another occasion, it was in the medicine cabinet inside a Band-Aid box. To an outsider, this probably seems funny, but I am losing my ability to see the humor.

One day, I leave the TV room, where Mollie and I had been watching "Everybody Loves Raymond," one of her favorite shows. Although she has trouble following any plot, she thoroughly enjoys the "one liners." She particularly likes the love/hate relationship between the mother-in-law and the daughter-in-law. I often wonder if she sees us in that position. Interestingly, the mother-in-law always seems to win.

When I return, I realize that my glass of chardonnay has disappeared.

"Mom, what happened to my wine?"

"Well, I certainly didn't take it. I don't even like that stuff."

I leave the room and back-track my route to the kitchen and laundry room, but find nothing. I am thoroughly perplexed. Three days later as I am dusting, I find it sitting behind the clock on the mantel. I know who put it there, but I wonder why.

She also always pesters me to let her do the ironing. I am afraid that she will leave the iron on the clothes, or worse yet, burn herself, but sometimes I relent if I am going to be close by to keep an eye on her. She especially loves to iron Bob's clothes. I think it brings back memories of ironing for her husband. Since she has a hard time remembering which parts of the garment she has ironed and which she hasn't, I have to check that both sleeves of shirts and both legs of pants have been ironed. She also has a weird preoccupation with pants hangers.

"Why, aren't these things clever?" she remarks as she opens and closes one over a fold in her blouse. She is sitting in her chair, and I have just put all the rest of the ironing paraphernalia away.

I try to take it, but she won't relinquish it. "We never had these when I was a girl. Has Bobby ever seen this thing? He would love it."

"I imagine he has," I reply, trying to figure out how to distract her. I am becoming a little weary of her animated interest in the darn thing. I set a cup of coffee on the table next to her along with a plate of tea cookies. She puts the pants hanger down to take a cookie and I quickly pick it up and set it on the table behind her, out of eyesight. This works great and she seems to have forgotten it. She puts her finger in the hole of the cookie and starts spinning it around with her other hand.

"Oh Mom, you're worse than my grandkids. Eat your cookie, and stop playing with it." Her antics are getting to me. I know in my heart that Mollie is just trying to be cute, but I am tired of it. I've had it.

The tragic part of trying to correct this type of childish behavior in an older person, who has dementia, is that you know that it will never improve or change; it will only get worse. Unlike raising a child, there is no hope that your teachings or reprimands will ever come to fruition. Besides, it feels weird and demeaning to correct someone that you have viewed as a role model for so many years. I don't like the person I feel myself becoming.

Later that evening when I go into her bedroom to tuck her in, the pants that she was wearing are neatly fastened to the pants hanger, which is hanging merrily from the ceiling fan, making lazy pirouettes as it spins around. In spite of myself, I smile.

Mollie is solemnly saying her prayers and probably asking God to look after her wonderful son Bob and his mean wife.

Another example of Mollie's inability to recall instructions has to do with the floor lamp that we had bought for behind the chair in her room. Bob wired it so that it could be turned on from the light switch on the wall, so that Mollie would always have a light when entering the room. At first she would turn it off at the lamp, so Bob removed the switch from the lamp. Next, she unplugged it in order to turn it off. At that point we put a post-it note on the plug which said:

"Please do not unplug me. Turn me on or off at the switch on the wall."

This seemed to work for a while, but then one day when I flipped the switch and the light didn't go on, I was stymied. It was still plugged in and there was no lamp switch, how had she turned it off? After going slightly crazy, I realized that she had unscrewed the bulb. This was a battle that we would never win.

As time goes by and the daily routine sets in, I must accept that I am not the loving person I envisioned myself to be. I remembered saying to Bob in the past, before Mom came to live with us, "Why does Mary have to be so short with Mom? What difference does it make if she doesn't do everything like Mary wants her to?" But now, I find myself feeling exactly like Mary must have felt.

Mollie will not put her dishes in the dishwasher, choosing instead to rinse them off (without using soap), dry them with a hand towel, and put them back in the cabinet...any cabinet. I once searched the kitchen for twenty minutes looking for my cookie sheet, finally locating it under the sink counter in back of the garbage pail.

I don't know why I can't seem to accept that the poor woman's mind doesn't work normally anymore. She can't help it, but it drives me crazy, and moreover it makes me angry. I want to see the humor in the things that Mollie does. I want to find her endearing, but I just can't, and I don't understand why.

She is enthralled with the laundry room. She loves the folding table and the rack on which to hang shirts and blouses. Almost every day, she goes into the laundry room looking for clothes to fold or hang up. This seems as though it could be very helpful, but unfortunately she stops the dryer mid-cycle and removes all the wet clothes. She then proceeds to neatly fold or hang them while they are still wet. No amount of explaining seems to change this behavior.

I try to avoid it by getting all the laundry finished before she arises. Mary's admonitions about Mom ring in my ears every time I hurry to complete this task. *"If you're smart, you'll take advantage of her sleeping late to get things done, because once she's up, she'll want to help you with everything, and she can't do anything. I know that sounds mean, but if you let her help you, it'll take you twice as long and frustrate the shit out of you."* She was right about that.

Interestingly, I never divulge these feelings to Mary, Kathy or Kristie. Whenever they call, I act as though things are just wonderful and their mother is a delight. Somehow, I want them to feel that I am the wonderful, patient caregiver that I thought I'd be. I realize the dishonesty of this, but I do it anyway.

CHAPTER 14

— ❧ —

Fascination
Nat King Cole - 1957

MOLLIE HAS ALWAYS had a fascination with gay people; and my hairdresser, Steve is as gay as they come. His main claim to fame is that he can impersonate Patsy Cline to a level that is almost frightening. He entertained at Bob's 60th birthday party in a pink sequined dress. I don't know exactly how he achieved it, but he had quite enviable cleavage. His legs made all the women in the crowd vow that they would double up on lunges and leg lifts. When he sang *"Sweet Dreams"* at the end of his repertoire, he brought tears to the eyes of even the most homophobic of men. That event took place over four years ago and people in attendance still talk about Steve. I really wish Mollie could have seen his performance.

Although I find that I am not doing all the things I had envisioned with Mom, I always take her with me to the hairdresser. Steve accommodates me by doing her hair at the same time that mine is scheduled, and this works out great for me.

Mom loves Steve. She can't remember the names and faces of her children or grandchildren, but whenever I mention Steve, she rolls her eyes and hangs her wrist limply, saying, "Oh, are we going to see Steve today?"

I find Mollie's view of homosexuals rather puzzling. Most religious people take a hard line on that issue and have little tolerance for their life style. Mom does not hold that viewpoint. She believes that they were born the way they are and had not chosen their lifestyle, which she views as a hardship. She has much greater disdain for George W. Bush than she does for gay people. She seems to have a gentle affinity for the latter, while no appreciation at all for "Dubya

When the subject of gay people arises, Mollie shakes her head and says, "I don't know why people have to be so mean. Those poor people didn't ask to be that way. They have a hard enough life without people being cruel to them. What if one of your children was like that? You'd still love them."

She enjoys having her hair done by Steve, even though the salon is physically attached to the back end of the County Line Bar. The first time I pulled into the parking lot, I thought she would faint. The County Line is a biker bar and you can imagine the reaction of an 88-year old woman to the tattooed men and their biker babes, clad in chaps and little else.

On this visit, after she has expressed her usual horror about parking next to the bar, I help her through the door. We are assaulted with the chemical smells of a beauty salon as we enter, and we are immersed in a beehive of activity. One stylist is razor-cutting the hair of her client with movements that would challenge an accomplished tennis player at Wimbledon. Every chair in the shampoo area is filled, and the hum of blow-dryers and conversation is quite loud. This scene always makes me think of the movie *Steel Magnolias*.

The area toward the back of the salon belongs to "Jim, the barber," who cuts the hair of most of the farmers in the community.

The majority of these men view Steve as someone to steer clear of. They aren't mean to him, but they try to have as little interaction as possible. I get the impression that they are a little afraid of him. A grizzled old man in overalls sits in Jim's chair having a lively debate about farm subsidies with another man awaiting his turn. Jim snips away at the man's hair while every now and then adding his two cents to the discussion.

Jim is a large imposing man with a kind demeanor. He had some kind of medical condition during his formative years that caused his head and feet to grow disproportionately larger than the rest of his body. This, combined with his full shaggy hair style reminds me of the lion in *The Wizard of Oz*. I am always concerned that Mollie might make some remark about this anomaly, but so far, she hasn't noticed.

Steve sees us and swishes over to greet us. "Mollie, my dear, you look ravishing, as usual." He plants a kiss on her cheek, and she beams.

"We have to stop meeting this way. People will get the wrong idea." She gives him a knowing look and winks. He laughs and gets her seated in a chair, while he directs me to his station.

"She is just the sweetest thing." He says as he wraps a cape over my shoulders and proceeds to apply my color.

Mollie is sitting quietly in a chair, waiting for Steve to finish my cut and color. Every now and then, she looks up and says, "Why Sherry, when did you get here?"

Steve chuckles every time she says this. He chides me for not having more patience when I groan.

When it is Mollie's turn, we trade places and Steve begins cutting her hair and singing to her. He is singing "*Down by The*

Old Mill Stream" and Mollie immediately starts singing harmony. They sing the song completely to the end and when they finish, all the patrons and stylists, who have stopped talking among themselves in order to listen, give them a standing ovation.

"Encore, encore," they chant.

Mollie, who used to be painfully shy, seems to be enjoying all of the attention. Steve grabs his Patsy Kline wig off of a styling prop and places it on Mollie's head. He launches into his rendition of *"Crazy,"* and just as before, Mollie starts singing harmony. It never ceases to amaze me that she can remember both the lyrics and the tune to all of the old songs. When they finish, they are once again rewarded with a hearty round of applause.

Although I love to watch Mollie in her playful moods, I am nevertheless always on tenterhooks, worrying that she might say something really inappropriate about Steve's sexual orientation or Jim's appearance.

As we are finishing up our appointments, Mollie looks at Steve and says, "You are such a nice young man. Why don't you have a girlfriend? Don't you like the ladies?"

"I prefer men, but if you were younger, I would go straight, because you have my heart."

How can you not love this guy?

CHAPTER 15

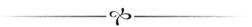

Don't Sit Under The Apple Tree with Anyone Else But Me
Glenn Miller - 1942

MOLLIE LOVES SITTING in the recliner in the family room where she can see down the driveway and also across the yard to Bob's workshop. Once as she watched him bustling about, she remarked, "Don't you think it's nice that Bobby lives right across the street?"

She enjoys walking down the driveway to the mailbox several times a day. She rarely gets any mail herself, although I have told everybody that she loves to receive it. Mary's daughter, Camille, sends her little notes with pictures occasionally and she always gets cards for her birthday, but that's about it.

"Sherry, is it alright if I walk down and check the mail? Do you think I need a coat?" she asks for the third time that day.

"It's warming up so I don't think you need a coat, but watch out for cars on the dirt road. Those people down the street drive way too fast." I encourage this activity, because it's about a tenth of a mile down the pine-needle driveway, and I feel that the walk is good exercise for her.

I watch her make her way slowly down the drive, swishing her cane at the Spanish moss that has fallen from the oaks, stopping to check out a flower or just staring up at the cloudless blue sky. I was warned that some Alzheimer's patients wander or try to "go home" (usually to their childhood home), but Mollie has never done that.

I wonder if Mom's desire to check the mailbox might have been a throwback to the time that Dad was overseas during the war. I remember her telling us stories about that time in her life and how hard it was. Marriage is not easy under any circumstances, but having a spouse in a foreign country in a war zone seems to add almost impossible odds to its survival.

I think about one of the stories that Mollie used to tell about that time in her life.

She would get home to her apartment in Delaware after picking Bobby up from the nursery. She couldn't wait to get to the mailbox to see if there were any letters from Bob. As often as not she would be disappointed, but on some days there would be a package containing many letters. All of the mail was censored during World War II so oftentimes there would be sentences that had been blacked out to protect any classified information from being inadvertently disclosed. The letters were then photographed and reduced to a 4" X 5" page that folded once to fit in an envelope through which the recipient's address could be seen. The return address on the envelope read "War & Navy Department, V-Mail Service, Official Business" and the postmark showed the date and New York, NY. Mollie still has some of these in her possession.

One day when she followed her usual routine, she was surprised to find a regular envelope in Bob's handwriting with a postmark from Paris, France, but then she realized that the war had officially ended and the letters were no longer being censored. I remember how she told that her hands were shaking and she could barely wait to get into the apartment to rip that letter open and feast her eyes on its uncensored contents. As she fumbled to free the letter from the envelope, a photograph fluttered to the floor.

She picked it up quickly and there was her handsome husband in his uniform smiling out at her from in front of the Eiffel Tower. Her breath caught in her throat just looking at him. He had filled out a bit and he looked incredible. His eyes were all crinkly around the corners and his smile was slightly crooked. She said that she wondered if he realized that when he felt a little self-conscious, his smile was always crooked.

Little Bobby had been crawling around her feet on the floor and he was starting to demand a little attention, so she picked him up onto her lap.

She always talked to Bobby about his daddy and so she said, "Bobby, this is a letter from your Daddy in France, let's read it."

(Mollie still has the photograph and the letter and this is what it says.)

"Hi Honey,

Well, things are a whole lot better here now that the war is officially over. We had a real good meal last night of roast beef, mashed potatoes and gravy, string beans, bread and butter, and cake and coffee. I don't know where they got their roast beef. Guess one of the G.I. trucks must have run into a herd of cattle and knocked a couple off, but anyway it was good and quite a change from stew or "C rations" or salmon cakes. The French people are treating us like heroes or gods or something. It really feels great to be appreciated.

I wish I could come home as soon as some of the other guys, but they need me to drive the brass all over the countryside. I had Gen. Bennett in the jeep the other day. He was going to present an award to Gen. Thiele for meritorious service."

I can picture as she stopped reading to put little Bobby in his highchair and give him a Zwieback cookie to chew on. He was teething and a little bit fussy.

She said that she was wishing Bob had been a little more romantic and a little less interested in what he had for dinner; after all, this letter wasn't being censored.

She picked the letter back up and Bob went on telling her about the different management styles of the colonels, lieutenant colonels and majors he worked under. How one of them was always trying to lend the fellows money when it got toward the end of the month. He went on to complain about having to get up for reveille in the morning and then he told her that he lost half his paycheck in a poker game last month. He closed the letter with "Love and More Love, Bob"

Mollie said that her feelings were really hurt and not only that, she was angry. He didn't say anything even slightly romantic: Nothing about how much he longed to hold her after all this time; nothing about how his heart broke (like hers did) when he thought about how long they had been apart; not even anything, not one single word about little Bobby, his only child. And the part about the poker game just enraged her, when she thought about how she had to scrimp and how much she had to do without.

She told me that she slammed that letter down on the table and picked up the photograph. This time she noticed a pretty young woman sitting on a bench in the background. The woman looked as though she was smiling at Bob. Oh no, her heart cried out, please don't let him go over and take her hand after this photo has been taken. Please, don't let them stroll together under the shadow of the Eiffel Tower. Bob had said himself that the French people loved the Americans. Please don't let this pretty girl fill the empty space that I have left in his life.

She was almost sick to her stomach as these thoughts raced through her mind and she sank into the chair next to Bobby's highchair. She turned the photo over and there was writing on the back in Bob's neat script:

This is a picture of your old man in front of the Eiffel Tower. I swear I don't know the girl on the bench. . . Honest.   Love, Bob.

I remember years ago when Mollie told me this story and showed me the letter and photograph. We had been discussing a girl at my Bob's workplace, who I thought had a crush on him. I had been asking Mom how she thought I should handle it and complaining that Bob seemed totally oblivious to what I perceived to be overt flirting. She had told me that there were always other women who would try to steal one's husband and that the more I reacted, the more Bob would notice. I always had turned to Mollie for marital advice. She and I had had some pretty candid conversations, and I missed that.

Sometime later, I look down the driveway and she is nowhere in sight. I run out of the house, calling her name. Where could she have gone? She was only going to the mailbox.

I rush over to Bob's shop and ask him to help me search for her. He jumps in the golf cart and heads out to the mailbox and down the road. My heart is pounding a staccato beat that hurts my ears as I head for the dock. Mom loves to sit out on the dock with us in the early evening, but I don't think she would go there alone because she doesn't know how to swim and she is afraid of water... but what if she had?

I hurry out on the dock looking for any sign of her, peering into the water, which is fairly clear and not too deep. I see nothing out of the ordinary and heave a sigh of relief. I head back up the hill and meet Bob, who has not found her either. I get on the golf cart with him and we go down the road in the opposite direction.

As we round a corner, there sits Mollie in the neighbor's yard. She is pulling weeds and singing her finest rendition of *Sweet Georgia Brown.*

We both breathe a sigh of relief.

CHAPTER 16

Someone To Watch Over Me
George & Ira Gershwin - 1926

BOB AND I have a problem. Mom has been living with us for over a year now and during that time we have not gone anywhere together. Oh, a couple of times we got away for a quick bite of dinner at the nearest restaurant and were back in an hour. I would sometimes accompany him to Lowe's or Home Depot early in the morning while she was still sleeping, but we didn't dare leave her alone for very long.

Now, we have been invited to the wedding of the son of Bob's best friend, Walt. Jeff is to be married in Tampa. This occasion will be especially poignant because Walt tragically died two years ago. Jeff, who calls Bob Uncle, phoned and told him how important it was to him that he be there since his dad could not. We obviously must go, and I am looking forward to it.

As a result, it falls to me to find someone to come in and stay with Mom for the entire evening. I first call several caregiver services, but I just don't get the right feeling; then I see an ad in the paper and call the "adult companion" to come for an interview.

The woman rings my bell at the precise time of our interview. She is a no-nonsense type. She's wearing a drab brown, rather institutional looking dress. Her steely gray hair is pulled into a tight bun on the back of her head. She gives the distinct impression that smiling is a terrible waste of energy that would be better spent beating rugs, churning butter or shoeing horses. Her name is Ingrid.

It is eleven o'clock in the morning. Mom is sitting at the table having breakfast when Ingrid walks through the kitchen with me. I introduce them, and then Ingrid and I go into the living room. I have the uneasy feeling that Ingrid will be interviewing me rather than the other way around.

"Oh," says Mom, loudly from the kitchen, "Ingrid is such a pretty name. I know a little song about a girl named Ingrid, but she was a naughty girl, would you like to hear it?"

"Not now, Mom," I holler back. "Ingrid and I need to talk for a few minutes." I am wondering to myself how Ingrid would react to the song, which I have heard many times before. It involves a rather loose woman and a number of sailors. I don't think this Ingrid would find it amusing.

Mollie shouts again, "You look like you're one of those Amish girls. I knew a girl in New Jersey who was Amish." Ingrid sits erect in her chair and acts like she hasn't heard a word.

As we begin our conversation, she volunteers that she noticed that Mom was drinking coffee, and didn't I know that coffee caused older people to lose their memory. Perhaps if she was in charge, she would see to it that Mollie drank herbal tea instead. As she talks, she pulls her resume from her Mary Poppins- type satchel and shakes it at me.

"You will see in this resume that I have cared for a great many older people and they all were in much better health after I left," she inhales deeply through her nose, making a little squeaky sound. I find myself wondering about the spirits of those healthy elders under the care of such a rigid person. As I glance at her resume, I see that she has not worked for anyone for longer than five weeks, so I assume that her powers are quite extensive ... or maybe no one can stand her any longer than that.

I quickly come to the conclusion that Ingrid would stifle Mollie's happy spirit in no time.

"Ingrid, we're not really looking for someone to stay with Mollie on a permanent basis. We only want someone to take care of her while we spend an evening in Tampa at a wedding. We'll be back the following morning, so it will only be necessary to fix her lunch and dinner. She probably won't even be up when we get home the next morning; she sleeps late and..."

She interrupts, "That is the worst thing you can let an older person do." I notice shiny little drops of spittle at the corners of her mouth. "These people must have a purpose in life. You must get her up at seven o'clock every morning. Fix her a bowl of oatmeal with herbal tea. Get her outside walking up and down the driveway by seven-thirty. Also, I hope you don't bathe her too often, as that will dry her skin out."

I notice that Ingrid's skin looks quite scaly and dry, and I wonder about her bathing habits. I am trying desperately to find a way to interrupt her, but I am distracted by Mollie. She is singing her little ditty about the farmer's daughter and how "all the horse men-new-er". Thank God her name wasn't Ingrid.

I manage to cut short the woman's diatribe on how to care for an aging person. I tuck her resume under my arm and stand up, telling her that I have just begun interviewing and I will certainly keep her in mind. I lead her out the back door so that we don't have to go by Mom again.

This is going to be a more difficult task than I envisioned. I have another interview at two o'clock with a lady named Irene. I pray that she isn't from Nantucket.

Irene arrives at ten minutes after two. She is dressed in a brightly colored muumuu. Her hair is styled in a loose, curly fashion, and she is wearing bright pink sneakers. She is a very heavy woman, and this worries me a bit because of Mollie's preoccupation with "fat people." I am worried that she might somehow hurt Irene's feelings by saying something inappropriate.

She was an art teacher in her working years, and when I show her some of Mollie's watercolor paintings, she offers to bring her supplies and help Mollie paint again. Mollie did many watercolors after she retired and was quite good at it. I have a number of them hanging in different rooms of the house. When Irene offers to help Mollie paint, the deal is sealed for me. I'd tried to get Mollie to paint again, but not having any artistic skills myself, it had not gone well. I hire Irene on the spot and decide that she can deal with the "fat issue" on her own.

After she leaves, Mollie asks me who the fat lady was. I answer that she is a friend of mine who is going to give her a painting lesson.

"Oh, that will be nice. I've always wanted to paint."

Irene and her husband, Mel, arrive at ten minutes after two on the appointed day. I asked her to come at one o'clock, but I am so relieved to see her that I don't care that she is tardy. She didn't mention bringing her husband, but at this point, I don't care about that either. He heads for the TV, and Bob gives him a quick lesson on operating the remote.

Irene begins setting up her painting paraphernalia at the kitchen table. She has even brought a plastic tablecloth. Mom is uncharacteristically quiet. She seems to know something different is happening, and she goes to her room and closes the door. I knock quietly and enter. She is sitting in her chair reading her bible. I feel as though I am sending her to be executed.

"Mom, you don't remember this, but I told you that Bobby and I are going to a wedding in Tampa. Walt's son, Jeff, is getting married, and it means a lot to him for Bobby to be there. This nice lady, Irene, will be staying with you until we get back tomorrow morning. She's going to give you a painting lesson and..."

"I don't want anyone to stay with me. I'm perfectly capable of staying by myself. Send them home. I don't want those people in my house." She shakes her finger at me for emphasis.

Wow. I hadn't expected this. I don't argue with her. I leave the room and go and tell Bob what is going on. He is always able to deal with her obstinacy better than I. He goes in and talks to her, and in a little while she comes out and greets Mel and Irene warmly. *How did he pull that off? I wonder.*

On the ride to Tampa, I am nervous about leaving Mollie. I think back to the time I left my oldest daughter, Tammy with a babysitter for the first time. I had been so excited when Bob suggested going to a movie, but I made him leave before it ended, and to this day, I can't remember what we saw. I picture Mollie crying bitterly, not eating her dinner and giving poor Irene a hard time all around. I beg Bob to tell me what he had said to her. He just smiles. *Why won't he tell me?*

The wedding is lovely, and I think about our wedding so many years ago. I squeeze his hand as they say their vows, silently reaffirming my own.

At the reception, Bob makes a beautiful speech about the happiness that Walt would have felt, watching his only son get married to such a lovely young lady. I'm really proud of him, knowing how hard it is for him to speak in public.

Walt's widow, Joyce, is very appreciative and begs us to stay overnight, but we had mutually agreed that we were worried about Mollie. We decide to limit ourselves to one glass of champagne so that we can make the long drive home. We arrive a little after midnight. Mollie is in bed, and Mel and Irene are snoring loudly in the recliners with the TV blaring. We pay them and they leave quickly. Irene has already packed her art supplies into the car, but she leaves the pictures that she and Mollie painted. I really think that Mollie's is the better of the two and so does Bob.

The next day I show the two sunflower paintings to Mollie, being careful to cover the signatures with my fingers. "What do you think of these?" I ask.

"Oh, Sherry, they're wonderful. Did you paint them?"

"No, you painted one of them and Irene, the lady who stayed with you painted the other. "Which one do you think is better?" I ask.

She looks confused. "I don't know how to paint, and no one stayed with me, but I do think the picture on the right is better. The shading and coloring are more realistic."

I remove my finger and there in the corner is the name "Mollie Bee." This was how she signed all of her paintings when she first took lessons. How did she remember that?

Later that evening after I have fixed Mollie's dinner and helped her get ready for bed, I go out to Bob's workshop. All I talk to him about anymore is the crazy things his mother has done. I tell him that she didn't remember Irene and Mel nor did she remember painting.

"You have to tell me what you said to get her to be civil to them," I say.

He sighs and says, "Why won't you leave that alone? If you must know, I told her that they were deadbeat relatives of yours and that it would embarrass you if she wasn't nice to them. She'd do anything for you; you know… she loves you."

I am touched by what Bob has told me. As I walk back to the house, I think about the rocky relationship I had with my own mother. I'm sure a lot of it was my own fault, but she seemed to hold me at an arm's length. I was only seven when my father died in a tragic accident. My mother was left with my two brothers, one who was a thirteen month old infant, the other, a two and a half year old toddler, and me. She had little money and few resources and she struggled to keep us all together. Prior to her marriage, she had worked as a trapeze artist in a traveling circus; swinging and doing jumps and tooth-swivels from a small plane mounted on a tower eighty-four feet in the air with no net; so she certainly wasn't lacking guts (although good sense might have been in short supply.)

After my dad's death, she moved us all from Kalamazoo, Michigan to Miami, Florida to be close to her parents. They were not in a position to help her financially, but at least they could give her moral support. She got a job running an elevator in a hotel on Miami Beach, and while she worked the night shift, it was left to me to take care of my younger brothers, who were then three and five. I remember standing out in the street late at night, watching down the road to the main highway. I could see the lights of cars as they approached and I prayed that each one would be her dilapidated old Dodge and it would turn onto our street. It would pass and I would wait for the next one until finally it would be her, and then I would run into the house hoping she didn't see me.

One night the older brother Barry got a nosebleed. He started crying and I went into the bedroom that the three of us kids shared. I found him in his bunk bed in what appeared to be an ocean of bright red blood. He had had nose bleeds before, but nothing like this. I tried to stop the bleeding with cold compresses and by having him lean his head backwards off the bed. Nothing worked. I was sure he would die. I ran through the backyard and woke up the neighbors. Mrs. Sasso, the Old Italian grandmother, followed me back to the house and somehow she stopped the bleeding. She stayed with us until my mother got home from work. My mother was embarrassed and angry with me for involving the neighbors, but in my mind, I felt like I had saved my brother's life.

I had a really good relationship with my mother at that time. She treated me more like a friend and confidante than a daughter, and I basked in my self-importance. It was when she started dating the man who would become my stepfather that our relationship started to deteriorate. From my vantage point now, I realize that he was a good man. But at that time, I viewed him as a rival for my mother's affection.

Slim was a roofer. My mother had met him at a local bar owned by a Hungarian woman named Magda. Her daughter Ellen went to my school and they lived in an apartment above the bar. Like me, Ellen had no father. We became friends, and I frequently spent the night with her. By that time, my mother had quit her elevator job, and I didn't have to babysit my brothers anymore. The apartment was ghastly hot on Florida's summer nights, so Ellen and I would crawl out her bedroom window and sit on the roof to cool off. We were both about twelve years old then, and one of the other reasons we liked the roof was that we could eavesdrop on the adult activities in the tavern. There was no air conditioning in the bar, and on hot nights, they left the back door open to get the cool night air and some cross ventilation.

One night, I recognized my mother's voice saying, "Slim, any time you decide to leave your wife, Minnie, you can put your shoes under my bed." She laughed.

I was perplexed, "What does that mean? Why would she want some dirty old roofer's shoes under her bed?" I asked Ellen.

Ellen was far more worldly than I, and she gave me an in-depth explanation that horrified me, although I tried to act quite blasé for her benefit. I didn't enjoy sitting on the roof much after that.

Slim and my mom eventually married, and they began to go to bars almost every day, after he got off work. I was very disapproving and vowed to never follow her example.

CHAPTER 17

❦

Hot Time in The Old Town Tonight
Bessie Smith - 1927

MOLLIE LOVES TO be in the yard, particularly in our little citrus grove. She also loves to ride around the yard in the golf cart. Bob started a little ritual of taking her for a ride every evening just before dusk. I've really grown to look forward to this time because it gives me a break from her.

One of the pleasures of living in Florida is that winter is the time when the citrus is ready to be harvested. We have far more fruit than we can possibly use and so this year, I buy some colorful half-bushel baskets to fill with fruit and give to friends and neighbors. I show Mollie the baskets; some are red with green stays and some are green with red stays. She is delighted with them and can hardly wait to get on the golf cart and go with me to pick fruit.

The weather is mild and the sky is a robin's egg shade of blue that only seems to happen in the winter. We wind our way down the drive and are treated to a sight I only see once or twice a year. There is a flock of migrating Cedar Wax Wings, who have stopped to nibble on the bounty of loquats in the trees that line the driveway. They are very skittish and it takes stealth to get close enough to view the little red wax-like dots on their brown-ish-gray wings. They have yellow tips on their tail feathers and a black mask that gives them a slightly sinister look. I am trying to maneuver us into position so that Mollie can see them, but every time we almost make it, they take to the air in a simultaneous rush. Mollie finally gets a glimpse and is delighted to see their markings. They remind her of a song she knows about a burglar and an old maid, and she sings it at the top of her voice.

My neighbor Carol has offered to come over to help us, and just as we get out of the cart and begin to pick the fruit, she comes down the driveway. Mollie loves having an audience, and Carol enjoys Mollie's wit. Some of the trees are heavily laden with large, plump grapefruits. The orange and tangerine trees look almost as though someone has decorated them for the holi-days with a multitude of yellow and orange fruits adorning the shiny green leaves. We make quick work of filling our containers. Carol notices the loquat trees and she asks me about the little golden fruits hanging in clusters.

"Oh, Carol," I say, "if you've never eaten a loquat, try one. They're really delicious. Just be sure to get a female fruit, they're sweeter and generally bigger, and the seeds are larger and more easily removed."

"You're putting me on," she says. Are you telling me that one tree has fruits of both sexes on it?"

"Yeah, really, the female fruits are rounder, slightly larger and much sweeter."

Carol cocks her eyebrows, looks at Mollie and asks "Is she kidding me?"

"No, she's not," Mom replies earnestly. "There are definitely both sexes on the tree and let me tell you … at night there is a lot of giggling." Carol and I dissolve into giggling fits ourselves. Mollie can be so witty and cute.

Carol takes her share of our haul and goes home. Mom and I linger a bit longer in the grove, hoping the Cedar Wax Wings will return. As the afternoon wanes, it starts to get chilly and we head for the house.

We bring the containers of fruit into the house and Mom makes it her job to stand at the sink for hours, washing and drying it. She loves the baskets that I bought, and she fusses with arranging the fruit in a pleasing manner. She appreciates the contrast of the orange and yellow citrus with the basket color, and she seems to stay focused on this particular task. She counts each orange, grapefruit and tangerine to make sure each basket contains an equal number. She is tireless.

I wonder what it is about this activity that keeps her on track.

She can't wait to distribute our gifts to the neighbors. I wonder if it is the anticipation of doing something for other people that has helped Mollie stay focused. I think about the unselfish, giving person she has always been.

I remember when she was a Girl Scout leader in Miami. Mary was in her troop and all of the girls envied Mary because her mother was so much fun to be around. She treated all of her Scouts with respect and never made them feel insecure when they couldn't accomplish some of their assignments. She would take the girls that were falling behind and spend much of her own time working with them until they caught up with their peers. Several of her scouts still send her Christmas cards and one of them brought her husband here to meet Mollie.

Maybe, even after a person develops dementia, there is an underlying part of their core that tries to revert to what it was in the past. Mollie has always been such a giving person. I'd like to think that part of her is still there. As I watch her filling the baskets with fruit that she has picked and washed, she seems like the "old Mollie" that I miss so much.

CHAPTER 18

It's Beginning to Look A Lot Like Christmas
Bing Crosby - 1942

BOB AND I have had a long dialogue about our plans for the holidays. Both of our children live out-of-state, and in past years, we would all gather at one of their houses for our Christmas celebration. It was such fun to watch our grandchildren open their gifts, and I was always very involved in holiday meal preparations. Since the kids cannot come to Florida this year, and it would be too disruptive to take Mom with us, we decide we will have to stay home.

We buy a small tree and I drag out all my decorations. Mollie always loved Christmas. I remember her spending hour upon hour, hanging the ornaments just so. She always built a miniature village under her tree and I remember how my children used to play endlessly with the same "villagers" that their dad had played with as a boy. There was a little skating pond made from a mirror, with ducks, geese and miniature skaters bundled up against the cold. I don't have nearly as complete a village as Mollie had. "Do you remember your Christmas village?" I ask.

"Oh, I was too poor for anything that fancy."

"I don't mean when you were a girl. You had a wonderful village when your children were young, and after they grew up,

Mary's children and mine, and then Kristie's played with it also. It was magical. You built a lot of it yourself," I say.

I can tell that she doesn't remember anything about it. How can that be? It makes me so sad.

Mollie seems to enjoy decorating our tree and I try to find pleasure in that, but I want her to remember and so I hold up a figurine of a little boy bundled up in a snowsuit and reaching out to throw a snowball. "You had a little boy much like this and you always positioned him aiming his snowball at the postman. I always thought that was funny, do you remember?"

She shakes her head no and stares blankly at the little boy.

As Christmas nears, we are invited to attend a concert of Christmas music at our friends' church. Jack and Jean were emphatic about including Mollie in their invitation. It is chilly when we arrive and I worry that Mollie will not be comfortable. A stage has been set up in the courtyard. The concert consists of two parts; one is contemporary music, which is unfamiliar to us. The second part is all of the traditional carols, and Mollie loves it. I feel a surge of love as I watch her face as she sings along in perfect pitch. I look over Mom's head at Bob and our eyes meet. He too is getting great pleasure out of watching and listening to her. Our friends, who are familiar with Mollie's condition, are astounded at her total recall of tunes and verses. They keep telling her what a wonderful voice she has. She revels in the compliments and attention, and keeps making little curtsies at the end of each song.

After the concert, Jean suggests that we go to Carrabbas Restaurant for dinner. Usually Mollie seems uncomfortable in a restaurant, but this time she seems relaxed and fits right in. She tells everyone little jokes that she remembers and even sings a little song. She is so animated, and I can't help but contrast her to the pre-dementia Mollie, who was very sweet, but a little on the shy side.

As we are leaving the restaurant, the hostess, who is a well-coiffed black lady with a wonderful demeanor, asks about the quality of our meal. She is dressed in a simple white blouse and stylish long black skirt. She wears a Christmas corsage of red and white carnations. Her fingernails, which are shockingly long, are all painted with Christmas designs; angels, Santas, snowmen, bells, trees and stars.

"Why, look at your nails," proclaims Mollie, grabbing the woman's hands for a closer look. "They are so beautifully decorated and they are so long." She smiles broadly at the hostess as she studies them.

"Thank you dear, I'm so happy you like them. She holds them high for Mollie to see.

"They must be great to pick your nose with," Mollie chortles.

The hostess is a bit taken aback; but without missing a beat, she replies, "Oh, they really are, but I only do that at home."

Our companions burst into laughter. Bob and I laugh too, but we are both a little embarrassed.

Christmas comes and goes. I am a little resentful at not being able to watch my grandkids opening their gifts, but Mollie is so childlike and excited that I get almost as much reward from watching her. The kids seem to realize my feelings and call more frequently.

I wonder ahead to next Christmas. Where will we be in our journey with Mollie then?

CHAPTER 19

Stormy Weather
Lena Horne – 1943

CHRISTMAS HAS COME and gone and a new year is upon us. It has been over a year since Mary went back to Texas and we have heard very little from her. I wonder to myself how she could have been such an integral part of Mom's life and then just cut it off; like a guillotine cleaving off the head of a ne'er-do-well. She never calls to see how Mom is adjusting, or for that matter, to see how we are adapting to our altered lives. This irritates me a great deal.

One evening after I have fixed Mom's dinner and gotten her settled in front of the television, I stroll out to Bob's shop to have a glass of wine and hang out with him. The phone rings shortly after I settle into a chair. Bob answers it with his usual jovial manner. "Mary, it's great to hear from you. We thought you'd vanished from the face of the earth."

I hear him take a deep breath with a slight catch at the end. "Oh, I see. I don't know what to say. Is there any chance they may have made a mistake?" He drops onto a stool next to the phone, as though he doesn't trust his legs anymore.

I see tears well up in his blue eyes, and the funny slant that his eyebrows take when he is struggling to maintain his composure.

I just listen to his end of the conversation, but I know something bad is coming.

He finishes talking to Mary and tells her he will call her back tomorrow night. "I love you," he says. "You'll always be my baby sister and we'll get through this together."

After he hangs up, I wait anxiously for him to tell me what's happening. After what seems like an interminable amount of time, he walks over to me and puts his hand on the back on my neck. He takes a ragged breath and says, "Mary has been diagnosed with pancreatic cancer. They've given her six months." The words spill out of him, running together, as though he wants them out of his mouth and out of his mind.

I didn't expect this kind of news. All I can think to say is, "Who's taking care of her? Where is she living?"

"She's staying with that Carlos guy."

"Bob, first of all, if she's that sick, she needs to be with her family, not some guy she met in a bar. He's just another in the long string of loser boyfriends she's had since she and Chet divorced."

Suddenly, I think about Mollie. "Just how do you think all of this is going to affect Mom? As far as I'm concerned, she's the major ingredient in this equation. I love Mary, but right now my main priority is your mother. Besides, you know how Mary always goes to quack doctors. How do we know that this is not just another drama in her life?" I feel unreasonably angry with Mary for foisting this news upon us.

Bob looks at me as though he's never seen me before. "How in the hell can you sit there and spew out your ridiculous speculative opinions at a time like this? My fifty-six year old sister, whom I have loved and been a big brother to all my life, has just told me she is dying in six damned months, and you're trying to micro-manage her last days. Who are you anyway?"

I am stunned and speechless. *He's right, my God, where is my sensitivity? I have known and loved Mary since she was nine years old and she's just told us she's dying. What's the matter with me? What have I become?*

I mumble something about checking on Mom and skulk out of the shop, across the yard and back to the house. I feel the heat rising in my cheeks.

I enter the house to find Mollie watching *Jeopardy.* "I heard the phone ring," she says. "Has anybody heard from Mary lately?"

This question almost knocks me to the floor. Mom has hardly mentioned Mary since she left. She always acts confused when I mention her. Why in the world would she ask about her now? It's almost as if she has a sixth sense. It makes me wonder if there is some kind of telepathic communication between a daughter in crisis and her mother.

I mumble something about one of Bob's friends calling and head for my office. My head is reeling as I try to assimilate the news we have just received. I'm not sure how to act or what to do. I decide that the best thing I can do after my outburst is to just keep my mouth shut and do whatever I can to show my support. I get on-line and start checking flights from McAllen, Texas to Orlando. I print out the schedules and take them to Bob. He looks at them and then at me, but neither of us says anything.

Finally he says, "You must have been reading my mind. I want to invite Mary to come and stay here. We can help oversee her treatment and get the straight scoop on her condition."

I'm ashamed to say that my first thought is how hard it will be to add Mary to the already difficult task of taking care of Mom, but I don't vocalize it. As I turn to go back to the house, he pulls me close and says, "I'm really gonna need your help through all this. I know that you love Mary as much as I do." We cling to each other for several moments and we are both comforted.

As I lie in bed that night next to my slumbering husband, my mind is whirling with thoughts of what lies ahead for Mary and for her family and us. I think back on her life and some of the tragic turns it has taken.

CHAPTER 20

Along Comes Mary
The Association – 1966

MARY WAS THE second child born to Bob and Mollie. She was born in April, 1948 in Pennsville, New Jersey. She was christened Mary Lee Turner and her mother was ecstatic that she now had a little girl in addition to Bobby, her beloved little boy. She and Bob would eventually have two more daughters, Kathy and Kristie, and all of them would be seven years apart. Mollie referred to the spacing of her children as "the seven year itch."

Mary always seemed to me to be "the tragic hippie." When I met her, she was a chubby, awkward nine-year old. She was brilliant in school and always had a special affinity for the underdog. She had made it her mantra to defend and fight any injustice, both real and perceived.

I remember taking her horseback riding when she was about thirteen. She was infuriated that the rental horses had to stand in the sun and that the handlers would whip them if they didn't go fast enough for the patrons. Short little Mary walked right up to the owner, a bearded, evil-eyed cowboy, who looked like he had just walked off the set of *High Noon*, and threatened to report him to the SPCA if he didn't start treating his animals better. I was admiringly shocked by her audacity.

When Mary started college, she moved out of the house and took an apartment with another girl, because she wanted to find out what it was like to struggle and suffer a little. I remember Mom saying, "If I had known she wanted to suffer, I would have thrown cold water on her every morning."

Mary met Chet, who was studying Finance. His family owned a bank in Tennessee, and it was expected that he would one day take over the family business. It wasn't long before Mary was pregnant, much to her mother's chagrin.

The couple moved back to his hometown and got married. Mary began her new life in a close-knit little town where she had no family or friends. Mollie worried about her continually.

Chet had always wanted to be a farmer, and not long after their little girl, Jody Lee, was born, he quit the bank and started farming on his grandfather's old family homestead.

Mary was now in her element. She grew vegetables in massive quantities, which helped feed the family and left enough to sell. She helped put up hay; she tended to the livestock; she became Mother Earth herself. She reveled in her new role of motherhood, imparting her somewhat unconventional views to her daughter, creating an intelligent, precocious little girl who was loved by all.

Mary did not view traditional housework as a high priority. She much preferred teaching her little girl to appreciate the wonder of a cocoon metamorphosing into a vividly colored butterfly, or learning to tell the ripeness of an ear of corn by the color of its silk tassel. There frequently were dirty clothes on the porch, piled to the ceiling; dishes often sat in the sink for days, and although she was a great cook, she sometimes had to search through the giant stack to find things to hastily wash prior to serving a meal. But that was Mary and this was the life she wanted to live. Her happiness was complete.

Mary and Chet had been trying to have another child without success, so Mary went to a fertility clinic and after several attempts, they conceived and had another child, Camille Hope (named after Mary's doctor). Camille was just beginning to walk when life changed forever for her family.

One day in early September, Chet and Mary, who was his best farmhand, were up in the hills, "putting up hay" when the little neighbor girl, who had been watching the kids, came running breathlessly up the hill.

"Miss Mary, Jody tried to get on her pony, Scooter, from the back, and he kicked her and she won't get up. You need to come quick."

I have often tried to picture this scene and feel what they must have felt: the horror coursing through their blood, the fervent prayers and promises to God that they both must have made during the frantic pick-up truck ride to the pasture, the moment when they first saw their beloved child lying still and motionless on the ground; the chaotic but fruitless efforts on Chet's part to fill her lungs with air and restart the heart of his precious child. And then ... more than any parent should have to bear, the deep, ragged despair that descended on them both as they realized that she was truly gone.

Mary told me in later years that they cherished the time they had with Jody in the field before the ambulance came. They held her and cried together. She said that they were resigned to the fact that God had wanted her back. She said that they had always felt that Jody had a special relationship with God and that he had been kind to them by not taking her before Camille had been born.

When she told me these things it was in an effort to comfort me. Bob and I had lost our third child, a baby boy at two days of age, but I was not so forgiving of God at that moment, and I flatly didn't believe her.

I will never forget Mollie's reaction when she got the news that her second grandchild, Jody, had been killed in an accident. At that time, Mollie and Bob Sr. lived in Miami, about ten miles from us. Bob's dad called to tell us what had happened. He said that Mollie had been out shopping when Mary called with the sad news.

He told us that he could barely get the words out. "When the car pulled into the driveway and Mom bustled into the room with her arms full of packages, I didn't know what to do. Before I could say anything she pulled out some fabric and told me she was going to make a dress for Jody to wear to kindergarten. She said 'She just started kindergarten, but if I get busy, I can have it finished and up to Tennessee in no time.'

He continued, "I walked over and took the material out of her hands quietly. I pulled her to me, but I couldn't say anything. The words wouldn't come. She seemed surprised by my unexpected hug, and asked me what had gotten into me."

He went on, "Just then, Kathy got home from school and I knew I would have to tell them both. Kathy gave me a peck on the cheek and started to tell us some story about her English teacher.

I couldn't help it. I handled it so poorly. I just blurted it out and hurt them forever. I've never had to do anything so cruel in my entire life."

He was grief-stricken himself, but he was also deeply worried about Mollie and Kathy. They both went into their rooms and didn't come out for days. They both knew firsthand the special-ness of that little girl, and neither could bear the loss.

Sadly, the loss of Jody seemed to be the beginning of the de-mise of Mary and Chet's marriage. Mary continued to function as "Mother Earth" on the farm, raising Silver Queen corn and taking orders from restaurants and folks wanting "fresh off the farm" produce. She would deliver two dozen or twenty dozen ears all across town.

She and Chet had two more children in addition to Camille; a son Brett and another daughter, Hannah. Mary helped the kids raise their sheep for 4-H, teaching them ways to wow the judges. But, even though we lived in a separate town, we could sense that the relationship between Mary and Chet had changed. There was no longer the closeness and there seemed to be an underlying tension between them that went on for years.

Once when we were visiting from Florida, we were watch-ing their son Brett, who was about eleven, helping transfer grain from the silo into the truck. The load chute had gotten clogged and Chet told him to climb up into the bed of the truck on top of the grain and unclog the chute. As soon as he got into the truck, the grain under his feet shifted and he went down into it so quickly that no one knew what had happened. He was there one minute and the next he had disappeared beneath the innocent looking kernels of grain. Mary screamed and Chet bounded up into the truck holding onto the sides as he repeatedly plunged his brawny arm into the ocean of grain, coming up empty hand-ed several times. Finally, he pulled Brett up, as though he had been propelled out of the mass by a spring of some kind. The boy was covered with the chaff and dust from the grain; it was in his nose and mouth and eyes. He was coughing and sputtering, but he was breathing.

Everyone cheered, except Mary. She collapsed on the ground, sobbing deep wrenching sounds, primal and animalis-tic. It occurred to me then, that I had never heard Mary cry, not even when Jody died.

The event with Brett seemed to bring Mary and Chet together again for a time, but soon they had drifted back to their seeming dislike of each other. When the kids were in high school, Mary decided that she would go back to school and learn to be a physical therapist assistant. I think she realized that she was go-ing to need a way to support herself. This decision put the final nail in the coffin of their marriage, and when Bob and I visited, they took us out to dinner and told us that they were going to separate. We were not surprised.

Mary now found the small town that she had adopted as her home turning against her. (I guess people always feel the need to choose sides.) Chet, after all, was a hometown boy, and Mary was a big city girl.

Their two older children were in college and their youngest was in high school, and in an effort to keep things normal, Mary agreed that she should be the one to move to an apartment. The town folk had a ball speculating about that, everything from

Mary being a lesbian; to her abandoning her children. She was undeterred and held her head high, but I'm sure she had some rough moments.

When Mary and Chet's divorce became final, and she had gotten her job certification, she accepted a job as a traveling physical therapist assistant, spending several months in one place and then moving to another. I think everyone in the family breathed a sigh of relief at her decision. Her new nomadic life style suited her, but once again fate was to deal Mary a card that none of us expected.

After several years of living in Texas and driving from one dusty little town to another, she noticed that she was having trouble with her central vision. She saw images in a wavy distorted manner. She went to an ophthalmologist and was told that she had an aggressive type of macular degeneration and would be legally blind by the end of the year. True to form, Mary took this news in stride. Although she could no longer drive, she continued working and functioning remarkably well. She never mentioned her blindness or let it keep her from anything.

We heard little from Mary after she moved to Texas. Most of the information we got came from Bob's mom and dad or from his sisters, Kathy and Kristie, all of whom were now living in Tennessee. Without the ability to drive, Mary was finding it harder and harder to get the jobs she was trained to do, and she had started cleaning and cooking for a couple who owned a bar. In return, they let her stay in a rundown trailer behind the bar.

The entire family was worried about Mary and it didn't seem as if her situation would get any better. This was around the same time that Mom and Dad were beginning to fail. Kathy and Kristie were finding it harder to keep an eye on them, even though they

lived fairly close. All of the family felt that they needed someone physically living in the house with them. Bob immediately
thought of Mary.

I didn't think Mary would want to move back to Tennessee, but
when Bob asked her, she readily agreed and everyone thought it
would be a good solution. At first, Kathy and Kristie were happy
to have Mary living with their parents, but as time went by, they
discovered that Mary came with her own set of problems. She
browbeat Mom about trivial things, and she and Daddy were
always butting heads. Kristie and Kathy began to resent Mary's
bossy nature, and they found that without her ability to drive,
they now had the added burden of having to take her every-
where she needed to go.

When Dad got sick and passed away, things got even worse.
Mary became even more inflexible where Mom was concerned.
For Mom's part, she no longer had Daddy to vent to, and she
seemed to always be nervous that she would do something to
set Mary off.

I think everyone was relieved when Mary decided to return
to Texas and we decided that Mom should come to Florida and
live with us.

But now she must cope with this.

—— ❧ ——

CHAPTER 21

How Can You Mend A Broken Heart
The Bee Gees - 1971

AFTER WE RECEIVE the sad news from Mary, we begin to put things in motion for her arrival. Although Bob has decided that she should come and stay with us, Mary has other ideas and flatly refuses his offer, at least for the time being. She stays in Texas for several months and calls every few weeks with an update on her condition, which is not improving.

I'm not sure how to handle this news with regard to Mollie. I call her neurologist and ask her if we should even tell Mom about Mary's prognosis. She advises us to tell her the truth in as kind a way as we can manage. I can't imagine any humane way to tell a mother that her daughter will soon die.

We try things like, "Well, we got a call from Mary in Texas."

She replies, "Mary? Is Mary one of my children? Why is she in Texas? Did I do something mean to make her go away? I think maybe I did."

Her responses always seem to stop us from pursuing the conversation further.

Mary helps solve the problem by calling one evening. I usually give the phone to Bob when she calls, but this evening he is taking a shower, so I answer.

"Oh Mary, I don't know what to say to you. I can't believe this is happening."

"For Pete's sake, Sherry, don't sound so frigging tragic. We're all going to die someday and we have to live in the meantime. Don't talk to me like I'm taking my last breath as we speak. Tragedy doesn't become you."

I am taken aback by her harsh response. I try to make my voice casual, "Well then, how the heck are you doing, girlfriend?"

"Well, that doesn't become you either, but let's get on with it. My kids want me to come up to Tennessee and spend some time with them; and to tell you the truth; I really want to see Mom again. I miss her." Her voice breaks, and I realize that her tough veneer has hairline cracks in it. "Anyway, I think I'm gonna get on the old dog and ride down for a couple of weeks. Then my kids can pick me up at your house and take me back to Tennessee. That way I'll get to see Mom and my kids. Will that work for you guys?"

"Of course it will, Mary, but you know that there is no way your brother will let you sit on a bus for that long in your condition. Let us book you a flight. I checked them out before and there's a direct flight. You won't even have to change planes. Bob will be so happy, he wants you close by so we can help you."

"I was hoping you'd say that." Her tone is softer than before. "Well, you'll have to get two tickets because Carlos won't let me travel by myself. He's really been helping me a lot. I don't know what I would have done without him."

This freaks me out a little. Carlos is Mary's Mexican boyfriend, and like all of the men in Mary's life since her marriage ended, he has let her control him and call the shots. If she is acquiescing to Carlos's opinion, she must be a lot sicker than I realize.

"Have you told Mom about me yet?" she asks hesitantly.

"Not yet, but she'll know before you get here."

"Yeah, she better... because I look like hell, and it will probably be a shock if she isn't prepared."

When Bob gets out of the shower, I relay the conversation to him. "Bob, you have to tell your Mom about Mary. She needs to be ready to deal with her appearance."

"Yeah, you're right. It's just that it's such a hard thing to do. I'll go talk to her right now."

I take a walk to give Bob and his Mom some time together. I feel like a coward, leaving it up to him to tell her about Mary, but I just can't do it and he handles things like this better than I do anyway.

As I walk down by the lake, I notice the beautiful sunset. The varied, ever-changing colors are reflecting off the lazy clouds into the placid water. It seems almost a garish display while we humans struggle with all manner of ills. I wonder how Bob is making out in his effort to tell to his mother our sad news. In spite of everything, I feel renewed when I return to the house.

Bob has told Mom the whole story. She has gone to her room and closed the door. I leave her alone and think of the way she had reacted when Jody died. The similarity is heartbreaking.

When Mom comes out for breakfast the next morning, she doesn't say a thing about Mary. I don't think she remembers. I find myself hoping that it will come back to her when she sees Mary. But, for the time being, she appears to be her usual happy self.

I think again that maybe Alzheimer's disease has a few good characteristics after all.

CHAPTER 22

Last Date
Floyd Cramer - 1964

WE MAKE THE arrangements for Mary and Carlos's flight to Florida. It's agreed that I will pick them up at the airport while Bob stays with Mom and tries to prepare her for Mary's appearance. As I stand at the arrival concourse, I think how much my life has changed since the last time I waited here for Mom and Mary. Who would have guessed this turn of events in only a little more than a year's time?

My thoughts are interrupted as I see them walking towards me. Carlos is a nice-looking man with a slight build. He wears cowboy boots that look like fishing waders because his legs are so short, and his long-sleeved striped shirt covers his fingers to the second knuckle. He has the ruddy, dark complexion of someone who spends a lot of time in the sun. His black eyes challenge his steely hair in their darkness. He is wearing a straw hat with a colorful band. He looks considerably younger than Mary.

Oh, but poor Mary. Her skin is a sickly yellow color and the gauntness of her face is almost macabre. Her eyes are sunken and huge in the smallness of her withered features. She is wearing her hair in a butch cut and wispy tufts stick out from her head like a scarecrow. Her clothes seem to be barely supported by her emaciated frame and she has a slight limp. But she still walks with a little swagger, and I know better than to do anything but give her frail body a gentle hug; and I certainly don't try to carry her small bag. I try hard to hide my horror at how bad she looks.

"Well, I told you I look like hell," she says as I struggle for something to say.

As we head for baggage claim, Carlos speaks his first words to me. "Is there someplace we can stop and get a case of beer on the way home?" I am taken aback, but I tell him I'll be happy to. They both sit in the car while I run into the liquor store and buy a case of Budweiser. I joke that we probably will all want one when we get home, and they agree; but other than a few polite exchanges, not much is said. Trying to make small talk seems irreverent under the circumstances and Mary's condition takes on the specter of the "elephant in the room."

As I pull into the driveway, the door to the house opens, and Bob walks quickly toward the car. Mary gets out, and though he tries to hide it, I see him recoil a bit at her appearance. I am hoping that her diminished vision keeps her from noticing. After hugging her, Bob goes to greet Carlos, but he is busily hoisting the beer out of the trunk and doesn't seem to notice Bob's outstretched hand.

As we enter the house, I see that Mom is sitting in her recliner, and I can tell that she is confused and doesn't know who they are. When Mary embraces her, Mom says, "Well aren't you the sweet one to give an old lady a hug?"

"Mom, it's me, Mary. Don't you know me?"

"Well, you do sound like my Mary, but you don't look like her." They both start to cry. My heart is breaking for everyone and I wonder if Mom remembers Bob's conversation about Mary.

They have planned to stay with us for three weeks and I fervently hope that Mom will get used to seeing Mary as she now looks. She has made the decision that she will not undergo any radiation or chemotherapy, and it has been determined by the doctors in Texas that she is not strong enough to survive the radical surgery that might have given her a few extra months. She opted to enroll in hospice services and was able to transfer them to a local chapter here. The hospice people will come three times a week and help her with the drain that is siphoning off the bile that her system can no longer process. They will also provide her with medication that will help with her pain.

Mary acts perfectly normal. She commandeers my kitchen and cooks one gourmet meal after another. She sits on the front porch with a pile of my cookbooks spread nearby, and with her magnifying reader she tries to find recipes that she wants to try. She holds the books up to the side of her face and studies recipe after recipe until she finds one that meets her fancy. She then gives me a shopping list and dispatches me to the supermarket. Sometimes, if the list is not too long, I take Mom with me to give her a break. It is during these times that she asks me questions that show me the depth of her confusion.

"Sherry, now tell me again who that lady and little boy are? Someone told me it was Mary, but I don't think it really is," she says.

Her obvious distrust of Carlos is apparent when she says, "I saw that boy take a bottle of something out of Bobby's liquor cabinet. Did you know that?" She has been calling Carlos a little boy since he got here and I realize that she is uncomfortable with him, because she has started locking her bedroom door at night. I have asked her not to, but to no avail. Bob finally has a key made so that I can get in to check on her.

"Mom, he's not a little boy. He's just kind of short. He's a grown man with grown children of his own. He came with Mary to help her. Remember, she's very ill. That's why you don't recognize her sometimes. We need to treat Carlos kindly. He's Mary's friend and he has been a great help to her."

I look over and see that she is beginning to cry. "I'm just so confused. I'm her mother, aren't I? I should be the one helping her, not some person that we don't even know. I just don't know anything, anymore and I'm no good to anyone. I should just die." She is crying harder now and shaking her head back and forth.

"Don't be silly. You need to stop feeling sorry for yourself; you know we all love you." I am being a bit sterner than I feel, but this approach seems to have worked in the past at nipping this line of conversation in the bud. I realize that Mollie is genuinely confused about Mary, but she has the sense that something is not right. I wonder if we should talk about it, but decide not to. She still seems a little pouty, but has stopped crying. "I just don't like having a stranger in my house. Where does he sleep, anyway?"

I had been hoping this wouldn't come up. "He sleeps in the bedroom down the hall." This was true, but it was the bedroom that he and Mary shared, and I knew Mom would be scandalized at that revelation. I hold my breath, but she doesn't pursue it. I distract her by pointing out a beautiful azalea bush laden with magenta flowers and we soon arrive home.

Both Bob and Carlos come out to help us unload the groceries and I notice that Carlos grabs the case of beer first and heads over to Bob's shop to put it in the 'fridge. Bob shakes his head and gives me his "what's with this guy look?" He helps Mom out of the car and into the house.

When we get settled, Mary tells us that her daughter, Camille, called and she and her husband would be driving down from Tennessee to take Mary and Carlos back with them. They have planned a big barn party to reconnect Mary with all of her old friends and relatives. Mary seems very excited about this, and I wonder if she is thinking that it might be the last time she sees everybody.

Camille and Curtis arrive the following weekend. Camille is as shocked by her mother's appearance as Mollie was, but no one comments. Her joy at seeing her grandmother and Mollie's delight and recognition of Camille take center stage and make for a happy moment.

They plan to stay with us for several days. Bob and I want to make their visit pleasant in spite of Mary's illness and the shroud of gloom it casts on all of us. Curtis is an assistant district attorney in their town and makes a hobby out of visiting courthouses in different cities. The old courthouse in Lake County is located in Tavares and was built in 1922. We thought Curtis would like to see it and have plans to take them tomorrow.

As we are on our way, Curtis tells us that he read that the courthouse was designed by the prominent architectural team of F. H. Trimble and Alan J. Macdonough, whose forte was Art Deco style. It has been included in the book, *Florida's Historic Courthouses* by Hampton Dunn. It is also listed in The United States National Register of Historic Places.

One of the interesting things about it for me is a bronze statue of a World War I "doughboy," which is prominently displayed in front of the building. It had been found in a field, covered with vines and dirt when the excavation for the new courthouse had begun. It is still a mystery as to why it had been discarded, but they cleaned it up and gave it a place of honor.

Mom loves it and talks incessantly about the fact that her father had served in World War I and had a uniform exactly like the one portrayed on the statue. This was an interesting bit of family history that none of us had known. Even Carlos seemed impressed. We visit the courthouse and then have lunch together.

On the ride home Mollie keeps talking about the doughboy statue. Camille, who is in the back seat, taps Mollie on the shoulder. "Mom-Mom, all this talk about the doughboy reminds me of the Halloween costume that you made for me when I was about six. Do you remember?"

"No I don't. Was it a soldier's costume?" Mollie asks.

"No Mom-Mom, it was the Pillsbury doughboy; and you taught me to giggle whenever you pushed my tummy. I think that was the best costume I ever had."

"I wish I could remember that. It must have been pretty cute," Mollie replies.

I find myself thinking how great it is that we can all act so normal, and almost forget the reason for their visit. Camille always had a great rapport with her grandmother and Mollie loves the attention and obviously adores her granddaughter.

On the day before they were to depart with Mary and Carlos, we decide to take everybody to lunch at Gator Joe's, a colorful old building that juts out over the waters of Lake Weir. It is located in the sleepy little town of Ocklawaha, whose main claim to fame is that it was the site of the shoot-out in 1935 between the FBI and Ma Barker and her son Freddie, both of whom were killed in the bloody battle that ensued. The shootout lasted over four hours, and it is said that it was the longest that the FBI was ever involved in. There are reports that a minimum of 1500 rounds of ammunition were poured into the house. We drive by this ramshackle old house before going to lunch, and everybody has fun trying to count the bullet holes that peppered the old two-story structure. Mom says she remembers hearing about the shoot-out on the radio. I wonder if that is true. When we park at the restaurant, she seems very nervous and doesn't want to go inside. I pull her aside and ask her discreetly what is wrong.

"Sherry, that's a bar. I can't go into a bar, it's not proper."

Mollie has always had an over-active concern with propriety. She wouldn't even rent videos of old westerns that Daddy would have enjoyed. She somehow connected renting movies with pornography. I'm sure Mollie has never set foot in a bar as a patron in her entire life, although she did have a job as a cocktail waitress when she was younger. I try to reason with her.

"Mom, it's a restaurant. They do serve beer and wine, but it's with food. We're going to all have lunch and we'll have a good time, O.K?"

She seems to relax a bit and says, "Well, I don't care what you say, I am not eating alligator."

"That's a deal, I'm not either."

Before we are seated, we walk through the building and out on the back deck, which is quite nice. There is a place where boats can tie-up while their occupants eat a meal or snack. There are about a dozen tables under a palm-covered structure and a walk-up bar for drinks. It is a beautiful warm winter day, the type of day that makes me wonder why everyone doesn't live in Florida. The water is very clear with an aqua tint that reflects the bounty of white, puffy clouds in the crystalline sky.

Several large ducks swim below and a feeding station is attached to the side of the dock, where a handful of feed can be purchased for a quarter. Carlos immediately buys duck feed and hands it to Mom for the ducks. This is the highlight of the day for her. She promptly stops talking about "not eating alligator" and enjoys herself. I am beginning to feel more kindly toward Carlos. Once we are seated and place our order, Mom begins to comment loudly about the other patrons. The restaurant is crowded and the majority of people are young retirees. I have no doubt that at almost ninety, Mom is by far the oldest person in the place, but she obviously doesn't see it that way.

"Will you just look at all these old folks laughing and carrying-on? It does my heart good to see old people having such a good time," she chirps. We all burst out laughing.

As we are eating, Mom asks Bob for his pen and begins scribbling something on her napkin. "This is what the two country boys said when they went out on that dock," She says as she holds it up and shows it to us.

M R DUCKS
M R NOT
O S M R
M R NOT
O S M R. C M WANGS
L I B M R DUCKS

When she reads it aloud, (reading the separated part as letters and the joined part as words) everyone is amazed. This was a riddle she used to show the kids. She always read it using a Southern accent. I find myself wondering how she can remember such a thing, when she can remember so little else.

The whole day is wonderful for us all, and it takes our mind off the fact that when Mary leaves, we will probably never see her again.

They leave for Tennessee the following morning and it is doubly sad because Mom is not yet up to see them off. Mary tiptoes into her bedroom to kiss her goodbye and I can tell she has been crying as she climbs into the backseat for the long drive. When Mom gets up several hours later, she never mentions any of them.

CHAPTER 23

—— ✍ ——

I'll Remember You
Andy Williams – 1964

SEVERAL MONTHS LATER, we receive the call that we have been expecting for some time. Mary's ravaged body has finally succumbed to the cancer she battled so valiantly.

She died with her children at her side and I'm sure she was surrounded by love. I was so proud that her kids rose to the occasion with such tenderness. Mary and Chet did a wonderful job raising them.

Bob is devastated and we talk long into the night. He seems to need to talk about Mary's life. We talk about her many roles: as his little sister; as the good mother that she had been to her children, and about how hard it had been on her when Jody died. We talk about her role as a daughter and as a caregiver to her parents. We marvel at her unbelievable strength and her resolution to not acknowledge the cancer that was rapidly turning her body into an emaciated shell of its former self. We marvel at the grace with which she had accepted her fate.

But we talk mostly about Mary as Mollie's daughter: the child for whom she had sewn ruffles on diapers, the chubby preteen who had excelled at building a fire without a match in her Brownie Troop, the rebellious teenager who had dragged us all to the showing of *"The Marquis de Sade"* in which all of the prisoners appeared buck-ass naked on stage. How in the world could we tell Mollie that her precious Mary had died?

I broach the question as delicately as possible, "Bob, you realize that Mom needs to know about this as soon as possible. We can't risk having her hear it from someone else."

"I know, but the thought of telling her tears me up. I'm sure she doesn't remember that Mary was even sick and I'll bet she doesn't have any recollection of her coming here to say her good byes. It will be like hitting her with a two-by-four."

"Would you like me to do it?" I ask, hoping he will refuse.

"No, this is up to me; and you're right, it needs to happen right away."

The next morning Mollie awakens at about eleven o'clock. I fix her breakfast and find myself hovering over her as she eats it; as though showing her extra attention might somehow soften the horrible blow to come. She is her usual chatty self, but I find it hard to respond to her questions.

Bob comes in as I am pouring Mollie a second cup of coffee and when I see him I feel physically ill. He sits down at the table next to his Mom and gently picks up her right hand, rubbing it against his cheek. I stand behind him with my hands on his shoulders, trying to show my support.

"Mom," he starts hesitantly, "we had some bad news last night. Camille called and told us that Mary passed away. All of her kids were with her, and she just peacefully slipped away from them. I'm so sorry to have to tell you this. I know how much you loved her. We all loved her." His voice breaks, and his eyes are glassy.

Mom pulls her hand away. She picks up her coffee cup and takes a sip. She seems to be gathering her thoughts, "Does Daddy know?" she asks.

"I think he probably does," he replies gently.

"Well, I'm just going to go to my room now." she says quietly, picking up her cane and shuffling through the kitchen towards her bedroom. We hear the door softly close.

"She'll be all right," Bob reassures me as he heads to his workshop, which is his sanctuary.

About twenty minutes later, Mom emerges from her room. She is whistling softly and I wonder if she remembers what has happened. She seems somewhat subdued and contemplative.

"Sherry, I think I'll walk down and check the mail. Is that OK?"

"Put on a sweater, it's a little chilly out there," I call after her.

It is mid-January and the sky is cloudless and the sun is blazing in the crisp winter air. The early blooming azaleas are almost iridescent in its light.

A great day for forgetting, I think.

I watch as Mollie starts down the driveway. She takes several steps and leans on her cane, looking up at the old dead pine that is home to so many birds. She shields her eyes with her hands, and as I follow her gaze, I see two large pileated woodpeckers perched on the side of the tree's trunk. They are pecking away the bark with powerful thrusts of their beaks. Mollie watches them for some time and then resumes her slow progress toward the mailbox.

She takes several more steps and bends over; as she begins to pull little dandelion-type weeds out of the grass, I can hear her talking quietly. I wonder if she is telling them about the loss of her oldest daughter. I wonder if she even remembers.

Perhaps she does, I think, perhaps she does.

CHAPTER 24

What About Me
Kenny Rogers - 1982

AFTER MARY'S DEATH, I find myself losing my patience with Mom even more than before. I am irritated by almost everything that she says or does. It especially bothers me that she seems to have endured the death of one of her children so easily. She doesn't even seem to remember Mary, and although I realize that it's because of her disease, it just reaffirms how much she has changed, and how little chance there is that she will ever again be the person that she once was. I become more accepting of that fact, but with that acceptance comes an overwhelming sadness.

I notice a progressive unraveling of my initial intentions to be a wonderful caregiver. I thought that taking her to concerts and events would bring her pleasure, and in truth, she did seem to appreciate the moments, but later when I asked her how she enjoyed a particular singer or scene, she would give me a blank stare or reply that she hadn't seen what I was referring to. Why am I going to all this trouble when she has no memory of the event? It seems pointless, and nobody cares anyway.

Mollie has become the only thing that I can talk about, either with Bob or my friends. I have become obsessed. Bob and I used to have great conversations on many varied subjects; now our conversations all revolve around "his mother." He points out to me that for all of our married life I called her "Mom," and now I always refer to her as "your mother,"… and not in a loving tone.

I am becoming somewhat paranoid. I feel an unspoken judgment on his part, a disappointment that I am not dealing with my role as caregiver in a way that makes him proud of me. I feel as though I am letting him down somehow and that I have not lived up to his expectations. I rarely see "Good Sherry" anymore. She seems to have given up and handed the reins to her evil counterpart.

Perhaps all of this is in my imagination. In my "before life," I would have brought it up, put it on the table to be aired and discussed. Now I am afraid to do that. Why? Am I afraid of the truth: that I have pretty much been a failure as a caregiver? Has "Evil Sherry" won this war?

I am hitting bottom. I feel that I am no longer attractive to my husband and I feel guilty about the manner in which I have been dealing with Mollie.

I am also drinking too much. I still go out to the shop to hang out with Bob in the evening, but more often than not, we end up in a fight. The more I drink, the braver I become in voicing my complaints about caring for his mother. I find myself saying mean and antagonistic things that I would never have said without the crutch of alcohol.

One evening after I have gotten Mom settled in to watch her programs, I go out to Bob's shop. He is working on a small entertainment cabinet for our bedroom. This project was at my request. In all of our years together, we had never had a television in our bedroom, but there are times now when I want to watch something that I am not comfortable watching with his mother.

Bob agreed, but wanted a cabinet that would conceal the set when not in use. He is almost completed with his masterpiece, and I pour myself a glass of wine and settle onto a stool to watch him apply the final coat of varnish that will bring the piece to perfection.

"Did you get Mom all settled in for the night?" he asks.

"She doesn't have her nightgown on yet, but she's been fed and she's munching on cookies while she watches TV."

I notice that I've already drunk my wine, and I go to the fridge to pour another.

"You put that away pretty fast," he says.

"Yeah, well I have to have something to look forward to." I counter. "We never go anywhere or do anything that's fun anymore." I notice his jaw tighten, but I am ready to let loose.

"You don't know what it's like. Your mother tells me the same story over and over. It's like being on a merry-go-round that never stops. I have no life anymore. You never hug and kiss me anymore. You never tell me I'm pretty or that you love me. I feel like an appliance or something. What's happening to us?" I slosh down my wine in a giant gulp.

"Sherry, you have to quit feeling sorry for yourself. You're always on the defensive. You're right about us, but it's hard to feel all warm and fuzzy to someone who acts like a rattlesnake. Where has my sweet Sherry gone? I haven't seen her in a long time." He walks over to me, stands behind me, and tries to hug me.

I jerk away, and he drops his arms to his side and sighs. I get up and storm back to the house, make a bee-line for the bedroom and throw myself onto the bed, pulling my pillow over my face. My inner voice is telling me that he's right, but that's not what I want to hear right now. I want to wallow in my self-righteousness, and so I do … for the rest of the night.

When I awaken the next morning, I realize that I have slept in my clothes. It looks like Bob slept on his side of the bed, but I'm not sure. I go to the living room, and he is reading the paper and drinking coffee. He greets me and I guess we're just going to act normal, so I follow suit. I feel as though talking might be a better solution, but maybe not.

I think about other changes in my life. When we retired and moved here, I formed a real circle of girlfriends. This was something that I had not had in my working life. Oh, I had several woman friends, but none that I did girl-things with. My new friends and I got manicures and pedicures; we worked out together; we took mini-vacations to fun places that our husbands didn't want to go; we met for lunch and went to movies. Since Mollie has come to live with us, my relationship with these women has waned and I feel abandoned by them. I don't know whether to blame Mollie or the rattlesnake.

I just can't find the joy in life that I have always felt. I don't even realize what's happening to me until I go for a routine doctor's appointment.

I have had the same doctor for many years. She's a petite woman in her early forties, who moves like a cute, little teenager. We have established a nice relationship through the years and have a genuine fondness for one another.

On this visit, she breezes into the room, gives me a hug, puts her hands on her hips and says, "Sherry, what is going on? Your lab report is terrible. Your cholesterol is up to 257; your blood pressure has climbed significantly, and you've put on over ten pounds. Look at you. You always looked so nice when you came in, and now you're not even wearing any make-up … and where's your usual smile?"

I'm taken aback by her frankness and I feel my face flush. I manage to stammer my response, "I'm wearing lipstick" I counter lamely, "but it seems so pointless. Why bother, anyway?" I am trying hard not to cry, but I'm sure the look on my face gives me away. I am not looking at her, but at the poster on the wall that depicts the various stages of osteoporosis.

She softens her tone. "Alright, I didn't mean to hurt your feelings. I'm just worried about you." She pats my shoulder. "I think you're burning out a little, caring for your mother-in-law, and you are showing classic signs of clinical depression. I want to put you on an antidepressant and see if that helps."

This is not what I wanted. I have always believed that life throws challenges at you and that handling them makes you stronger and builds character. I can't believe that caring for a sweet little old lady, whom I love, should affect me to this degree.

My response is a bit curt. "I don't want any 'feel good' medication. I think I can handle this by myself. You need to give me a little time, and I need to give myself an attitude adjustment. I can change things." I smile and nod my head for emphasis.

"Well, it's certainly your call, and I've known you long enough not to argue; but don't try to be a hero. Everybody needs a little help now and then. Talk to Bob, and see what he thinks. There is no stigma in taking medication for a documented condition. Will you think about it? Let's set up another appointment in three months. In the meantime, try to be kind to yourself."

She pats my shoulder again. I mumble my thanks as she leaves the room.

As I drive home from the doctor's office, her words, "Be kind to yourself" resonate in my mind. She's right. I vow to be less judgmental of myself. After all, what I am doing is difficult. Not only that, I promise to take more time for myself and pay more attention to my appearance. I will get on a sensible diet and stick to it. I can turn this around.

CHAPTER 25

There'll Be Some Changes Made
Benny Goodman - 1941

WHEN I ARRIVE home, Bob is sitting in the family room with Mollie. They are watching a rerun of *Bonanza*, and they both seem happy and relaxed in each other's company. *Why don't I let Bob do this more often? He is certainly willing. Why do I think I am the only person who can care for Mollie? I can't believe I am such a martyr.*

That evening at cocktail hour, I tell Bob what the doctor said. He agrees that we need to make some changes. He offers to take care of Mom more often and let me take more time for myself.

"I had some news today that might fit into this whole equation," he says. "Kathy and Trent are going to move down here. They'll both have to get jobs, but they're going to try and find a house close by. Kathy wants to help with Mom's care as much as her job will let her."

This is great news and I feel my spirits soar. This could really work. Having Kathy living nearby would make me feel a little less alone in my responsibilities, and maybe Bob and I could have a little more freedom and take time for ourselves. This news adds to my determination to make some changes. I have to accept that I can't fix what is wrong with Mollie, but I can fix myself and I vow to try.

My daughter Jennifer signed me up for a writing workshop several months ago because she, too, felt I needed an outlet. At the time, I thought it was a silly gift. I joked that she should have given me a pretty blouse instead. But this could fit nicely into my new plans. I have always wanted to write. Perhaps writing about Mollie will be therapeutic.

The next day I call and sign up for my first writing workshop. Jennifer is thrilled when I call and tell her. When I tell her about my doctor's visit, she confides that she and her sister, Tammy, have been genuinely worried about me. She says they have noticed a change in my voice and a lack of enthusiasm in general. She is glad I have refused anti-depressants, but happy that I recognize that there is a problem and that I am going to address it.

The day of my first writing workshop arrives, and I am filled with trepidation as I drive to the private home where it is to be held. What if they laugh at me? What if I embarrass myself? What if Bob has a hard time handling his mother? Am I doing the right thing? I have to fight the urge to turn around and go home. The drive takes me an hour and a half, and by the time I arrive, I am a basket case.

I find that the class is actually called a writing marathon and lasts an entire day. I know no one and have never met the coach. I have borrowed a laptop computer that I barely know how to turn on. There are about twenty people already there when I arrive, all of whom have participated in some form of this activity before and most of whom are considerably younger. I have no idea what to expect.

The host's home is very welcoming and nicely decorated. People are seated at tables and chairs, on couches and settees, and even on pillows on the floor. Some are using laptops, and some are writing with paper and pen. The setting is quite casual.

Everyone treats me warmly, and by lunchtime, my anxieties have abated and I begin to enjoy myself. The writing coach, Jamie, gives the group some type of prompt: a physical item, a situation, a poem, etc., that we are supposed to write a story about. She gives us a length of time in which to finish, and then everyone reads their story aloud, after which we hear comments from the group. The comments are supposed to be generally positive, but occasionally are constructively critical.

I have never written before, and I certainly am not very good, but I find that every prompt elicits a "Mollie story," and that people seem to genuinely enjoy them. I am blown away by the stories and the quality of writing of the group in general. Jamie seems to have a real knack not only for keeping the group on track, but also for bringing out the best in all of us. I find myself eagerly looking forward to the bi-monthly workshop to follow.

When I arrive home that evening I regale Bob with stories about the workshop and for the first time in months, there is no discussion about "his mother."

CHAPTER 26

You're So Vain
Carly Simon – 1972

Since my doctor's appointment and my realization that I have not been taking care of myself, things are changing bit by bit. I have been making a genuine effort with my appearance, taking more time with my make-up and dressing more attractively. I am trying to lose some weight and have had some success. The best thing is how much I find myself looking forward to my writing workshops twice a month.

Mollie is the same as she was, of course. She still asks the same question, repetitively. She still has no memory of recent events or even who her children are. She doesn't remember that her husband and daughter have died. She still makes inappropriate comments. I continue to have to monitor her every move: bathing her, making sure she wears clean clothes, and taking care that she doesn't get lost or injure herself. But somehow, by redirecting my focus on my own well-being, these chores don't seem as insurmountable as they did before.

Several months later, Bob and I are watching television, while Mollie is going through her photographs, when a really interesting ad comes on. It is a commercial for a procedure called The

Lifestyle Lift. *"Do something for yourself for a change"* says the moderator. The ad shows picture after picture of women *before and after* having had this procedure. It is amazing! I memorize the phone number and later that day I call for the informational brochure. It arrives two days later and it is unbelievable. There is a cavalcade of pictures of women who have had the procedure. Some are older than I, some are younger. There are pretty women and homely women. They all have been amazingly transformed. The lines and wrinkles are gone from their necks and lower faces; frown lines have totally disappeared; and every one of them looks at least ten years younger. The brochure calls it "<u>a real procedure with real results;</u> not a thread lift or a miracle cream; look years younger; takes about an hour with our technology."

This might be what I need to boost my sagging morale, not to mention my face. I am excited! I am sixty-four years old, and I can't tell you the number of times I've stood in front of the mirror and pulled my sagging skin up tightly next to my ears and thought Wow, *what a difference THAT would make.*

I remember watching Nora Ephron, the author of *I Feel Bad about My Neck,* on the Oprah show. She is a charming and attractive woman, wearing a scarf tastefully wrapped around the offending body part. She said that at a certain age (far younger than I) the neck just couldn't help but looking old; no matter what. *YES!* I think, maybe it IS time to *"Do something for yourself for a change."*

The next day, I show the brochure to Bob. He is impressed, but skeptical.

"I'm sure you must realize that this procedure is not a walk in the park; not to mention that those pictures have certainly been retouched. If you want to put yourself through something like that I won't object, but I think you look fine the way you are. Do whatever makes you happy."

Two weeks later finds me driving an hour and a half to Orlando, feeling like everyone is watching me and thinking, what *a vain, silly woman she must be.* I find my way to the waiting room and watch a clip of Katie Couric talking to several women who had done the procedure, one of whom said she and her daughter had actually gone to lunch afterward. Wow!

My counselor is an upbeat young woman who reminds me of a Barbie doll. There is nothing on her that remotely re-sembles a sag, wrinkle or jowl. The pluses enumerated both in writing and by Barbie are as follows: 1) Local anesthetic 2) Awake and relaxed 3) Natural results 4) Minimal bruising and/ or swelling 5) Takes about 1 hour 6) Return to work quickly vs. traditional procedures 7) Affordable for most everybody 8) Experienced doctors and staff.   They assure me that if I make the appointment today, I can cancel at any time up to 48 hours before the procedure. So, I talk them down $100 (such a bargainer, I am) and arrive home armed to the teeth with information for my hubby.

On the next meeting, Bob goes with me to meet the surgeon. Kathy has come to the house to take care of Mom. She thinks I'm crazy to even consider such a thing. The doctor explains that the lab work shows that I am a good candidate, health-wise, but he doesn't make it sound like quite so minimal a procedure. He ex-plains that there will be considerable bruising and swelling; plus, he gives me prescriptions for one antibiotic, a sleeping medica-tion, a prescription for nausea and hydrocodone for pain. That seems like a bit much for a walk in the park. Bob's main concern is that I not look "stretched and unnatural," and the doctor assures him that any stretched look would soon disappear.

The die is cast. My lifestyle and my face are soon to be lifted. I am not quite sure how to handle this. Who do I tell? Should I tell my friends and family? How in the world will I explain something so self-centered to Mollie? After all, she went through the Depression and never owned more than two pair of shoes at one time in her life. I decide to just play it by ear, and I keep trying to convince myself that this is something I need for my self-esteem.

We leave the house at five o'clock in the morning of the big transformation day. We make arrangements for someone to come in and take care of Mom, because Kathy has to work that day. The Center told us to be there at seven-thirty, as I am to be the second patient of the day. When we arrive, there is a man in the waiting room, whose wife is undergoing her second lift in five years. He says she looked fantastic after the first one. This information calms me a bit.

The medical staff is nowhere to be found. I chat with Bob about trivial things, but my inner voice keeps screaming, *Run! Run!* About an hour later, a technician comes out and introduces herself. She gives me three pills to take; one of which is a Valium, to calm me. Just before calling me back, the doctor comes out and tells the man that his wife had done just fine; and had actually slept through the entire ordeal. This is a good thing to hear! I kiss Bob goodbye, hoping it will not be for the last time, and they take me back to the surgical suite. I sit in a chair that looks like a tilted back dental chair. They put a drape over my clothing and it is off to the races.

Dr. Palliaci is a pudgy little Italian guy with a baby-faced somberness and a perpetual five o'clock shadow. He seems slightly vulnerable, and this makes me like him. For some reason, I picture him married to someone like Anna Nicole Smith, who bosses him around and makes his life miserable. I feel strangely protective of him.

My fondness for him begins to diminish when he proceeds to numb the entire perimeter of my face with a syringe the size of a gallon of milk. Dr. P's assistant introduces himself to me. His name is Boris. (Why am I surprised that it isn't Igor?). I am now definitely having second thoughts, and cute little Dr. P. is beginning to resemble Vincent Price in the Frankenstein movies.

As they are deadening my face, I suddenly realize I can't close my right eye. Boris calls "the eye" to Dr. P's attention and he calmly replies that "sometimes that happens." There is a brilliant light shining into an eye that will no longer function and I am surprised that I don't have the wherewithal to ask them to cover it with a cotton pad or something, but I don't.

As Dr. P. proceeds to practically remove both my ears and suck all the fat out of my neck, I think about frontier people being scalped by Indians, who did it for free. This is NOT fun! Perhaps, general anesthesia, with all its inherent risks, might be a bit more humane. As they loosen skin and pull it so tight that I think my bridge might pop out, I hear the distinct sound of my skin being cut with scissors just above my ear. That does it! Now I am beginning to panic. I keep moving my legs on and off the chair. Dr. P. speaks reassuringly, telling me that he is just about finished; then he tells Boris to go and get another Valium and put it under my tongue.

I keep trying to picture myself lying on a beach. The bright light shining in my eye is just the sun, and no one is removing my face after all. Actually, they are now sewing my ears back into place, and Dr. P. is telling me again that they are almost finished. They then wrap my entire face with a really tight Ace Bandage, wound around the top of my head, over both my ears and around my chin. I am instructed that this is not to be removed until the next day. After a short recovery period we head for home, and I just lean back in the seat and close my eyes. Bob tells me later that the people in the cars we passed did a double-take at the mummy in the front seat.

I hide out in the bedroom as soon as we get home and stay put until the next day when we return to the doctor to have the bandages changed and the incisions cleaned and checked. A technician does all that stuff; but one interesting thing is that they have a separate entrance into the suite for **"Post-Surgical Patients."** Ah Ha! That's to keep enthusiastic people like me from seeing the "real Post-Op People," who in no way resemble the "Brochure People." But, by now I feel that the worst is over.

The next morning after very little sleep, even with the sleeping pill and the hydrocodone, I go into the bathroom to brush my teeth. This is quite difficult, because my mouth will only open a very tiny bit. When I look in the mirror at the part of my face that is not covered with the Ace Bandage, I realize that I now have two beautiful black eyes and the left side of my jaw and chin look like Sylvester Stallone in *Rocky*. My entire face is swollen to the size of a mini-watermelon and my earlobes sticking out of the bottom of the bandage look like Dolly Parton's boobs after the most recent augmentation. Good thing I don't have to go to work on Monday like I'm sure some people in this same condition might have planned.

I seclude myself in the bedroom for three days, watching *The Godfather* marathon on TCM. I cannot eat anything more than pudding or soup, not only because my jaw won't open very wide, but also because it hurts to chew. Bob had moved to the guest room the first night, because as the swelling grew, so did the resonance of my snoring. He tries to come back the third night, but he still can't stand the din.

I finally decide that I can't hide from Mom any longer, and I start fixing her meals and socializing with her again. This is some-what traumatic for both of us, because every time she sees me in my bruised wonder, she starts to cry. I explain that I have had some jaw surgery and two minutes later, she notices my face and starts to cry AGAIN. It is really becoming tedious. At one point, she asks in a hushed tone if Bob (her only son and the sweetest, most gentle man in the world) had HIT me. I had not anticipated this reaction from her, so I decide that the more she sees of me, the sooner she will get used to the way I look.

I try to make my recuperation seem as normal as possible, but as I am lying on the sofa in the living room watching television with her, I notice that she is very quiet. I wonder what is going through her mind. Just as I start to comment, she turns to me and says in a very sweet little voice, "Where has Sherry gone?"

"Mom," I reply as nicely as I can, "Don't be silly, I'm Sherry, and I've been right here for two hours, watching *The Animal Planet* with you."

"Oh I didn't realize that was you." Several minutes pass and she leans over and says again, "Does anyone know where Sherry went?" Some things never change.

As every day my face gets a little better, she stops asking me that question. The bruises disappear in about ten days; the swelling goes down bit by bit and ever so slowly the benefits begin to emerge. I think my neck and lower face definitely look smoother and much more wrinkle-free. I don't have jowls any-more. My earlobes are slightly uneven, but all in all, I am glad I did it. I am anxious to see how my friends and family react, or if they even notice a difference.

Things seem to be looking up for me. I am definitely getting a little more time for myself. I am enjoying writing and reading to others about Mollie. Bob has been spending more time with his mother, and he has even agreed to take me on a trip to Ireland in September with friends of ours. This is really a stretch for him, and I know how hard he is trying.

CHAPTER 27

What's Love Got to Do With It
Tina Turner – 1984

IT HAS BEEN six months since Mary died and I have done a lot better in controlling my aggravation with Mollie's condition. Kathy and Trent have bought a house quite close to us, and even though they both have jobs, Kathy drops in every week or so with her Yorkshire terriers. Mom loves those little dogs and tries to feed them whatever goody she can find. I had hoped Kathy could spend more time with Mom, but with her job that was an unrealistic expectation. Even so, having her nearby does give me comfort.

On this particular morning as I watch Mollie eat her breakfast, I am filled with an unusual sense of happiness. After much trepidation and many negative comments from both Kathy and Kristie, I have prevailed and I am feeling the rosy glow of triumph. Today, we are taking Mollie on an airplane to Tennessee to watch Mary's son Brett, Mollie's cherished first grandson, wed the love of his life.

Brett and Tina have known each other since grade school. Brett always had a little crush on Tina, but in high school, she started dating his cousin Evan. Brett started going with another young lady and sometimes they even double-dated. When Evan and Tina got married, Brett was Evan's best man. As time went by, Brett broke up with his girlfriend, but always remained close to Tina and Evan. They had helped Brett a great deal as he tried to come to terms with his mother's death.

One morning after Tina and Evan had been married for several years, the unimaginable happened. Tina was awakened by the sound of Evan gasping for breath. He was only in his late twenties, but he was having a heart attack. Tina, who had studied nursing, did everything she knew to do, but by the time the ambulance arrived, Evan was gone.

Brett was as devastated by the loss of his best friend and cousin as Tina was the loss of her husband; neither thought they would survive, and each understood the depth of the each other's loss. They supported each other and over the next few years, their shared experiences deepened into love. Their families gave them their blessings when they decided to marry. We were all happy for them. The only sad part about this was that Mary would not be here to see their wedding.

"You're crazy. Don't you realize what you'll be doing to yourself?" Kathy almost spat those words at me when I first suggested taking Mom to Brett's wedding. "You'll go nuts trying to get her on an airplane, and not only that, you and Bob will be trapped. She'll ask you a million times where you are going and why. Are you insane? Just let me watch her. I'll come over here while you're gone and when I'm at work we'll get that lady you hired once before to come in and stay with her. Go and enjoy a little break from Mom while you have the chance."

What she said was tempting, but I really felt strongly that Mom should be there. I thought Kathy should be there as well, but she said it was too much of a hassle to get time off from work. That was her decision and not my place to argue, but I did argue on Mom's behalf. We hadn't taken her to Tennessee for Mary's funeral because we felt it would be too confusing and sad for her, but this would be a happy occasion with many friends and family who loved her and wanted her there.

"Kathy, this is not about me or Bob. This is about Brett and Mom. Do you know how much it will mean to him to have his grandmother at his wedding? Just remember, his mother died last year and so did his other grandmother. Mom is all he has left, and I think we owe it to him to take her. She can stay with Kristie, since she has a downstairs bedroom, and that will be nice too since Mom can't even remember who Kristie is now. This will be good for everybody, and we'll get a break since we'll be staying with Tammy." Kathy shakes her head and reluctantly agrees.

I lay out Mom's clothes and give her a bath before breakfast. Bob puts new batteries in her watch, which she always likes to wear when she is dressed up. I follow her into her room after breakfast to help her get ready.

"O.K. now, you get dressed." I point to the clothes on the bed. "Today is an exciting day. You and Bob and I are going on an airplane to Tennessee, and day after tomorrow, we're going to Brett's wedding."

"Brett's getting married," she says. "Why I can't believe little Brett is getting married. Who is he marrying?"

"He's marrying Tina," I reply.

"Tina Turner," she responds.

Where did that come from? I didn't think she even knew who Tina Turner was?"

"No, Mom, not Tina Turner. That's silly. He's marrying Tina Edwards.

"Now, hurry up and get dressed. I'll be right back. Oh, and Bobby put new batteries in your watch, so you can wear that too. It's on the dresser."

When I return to her room some ten minutes later, she is sitting in her chair thumbing through a book. She is dressed in a sweat shirt and an old pair of pants. Her lovely pantsuit is hanging neatly in her closet and her watch has disappeared from the top of the dresser.

"What are you doing?" I say, more harshly than I intend. "Why aren't you dressed and where did you put your watch?" She looks at me as though I have slapped her.

"What do you mean?" she asks.

"Mom, can't you remember?" *(Stupid question)* We have to leave for the airport in a few minutes. You were supposed to be getting dressed."

"Well, I didn't know that. What am I supposed to wear?" There is a peevish tone to her voice.

I snatch the clothes from their hangers and shake them at her. "These. They were on your bed."

I pull the sweatshirt over her head somewhat roughly. The voice of "Good Sherry" is screaming in my head, "*Get a grip.*" I take a deep breath and try to relax my shoulders. *Maybe Kathy was right*, I think for the first of many times that day.

In a more gentle tone, I say "It's OK Mom, I'll help you. We're going on a big adventure. We're going to Brett's wedding."

She looks a little happier now, "Little Brett is getting married? Who's he marrying?"

"He's marrying Tina," I reply cheerfully.

"Tina Turner?"

After the dressing ordeal, Bob gets Mom settled in the front passenger seat of the car. It is easier for her to get in the front seat, so when the three of us go anywhere, she sits up front with Bob and I sit in the back seat.

"You seem so tense." Bob says to me as I climb in back. "Why can't you relax and enjoy yourself a little?" I picture his beautiful blue eyes bugging out of his head as I strangle him, but I banish that thought and quietly buckle my seatbelt.

"Where are we going?" Mom asks Bob.

"We're taking an airplane to Tennessee. We're going to go to Brett's wedding," Bob answers.

Here it comes...

"Little Brett is getting married? Who's he marrying?"

"Tina."

"Tina Turner?"

I feel smugly vindicated when he says, "Mom, that doesn't make any sense. He wouldn't be marrying Tina Turner. Don't say that again."

Right.

We ride in silence for a little while and I feel as though Mom's feelings have been hurt. She is very quiet and staring out the window. She is very sensitive to Bob, so when he scolds her, it has more of an impact than when I do. After a while, she looks over at him and asks, "Where is Sherry?"

"She's in the back seat, right behind you," he replies.

For some reason, this makes me giggle.

When we arrive at the airport, Bob drops us at the outside luggage check-in area while he goes to park the car. A cheerful porter sees Mom get out of the car with her cane and bustles up beside us with a wheelchair. He is a very dark black man with a broad smile. He is chewing on a green and white striped paper clip.

"How you doing girlfriend?" he says to Mom.

"Well, I'm just fine." She points her finger at him and says, "I'll bet you know David Durham. He was a Negro who lived near me in Smyrna, Delaware when I was a girl. He was just about your age."

"Why I thought he was a famous Rap star," replies the porter giving me a sly wink. "Besides, all us good-looking men resemble each other."

I am worried that Mom might have offended him, but he checks our luggage in cheerfully, so I guess no harm has been done. I wonder again to myself why Mollie has such a weird way with black people.

Bob comes up from parking the car. He looks a little harried. Mom asked him at least twenty times where we were going on the ride to the airport, and he reached the point where he didn't mention Brett's wedding because he didn't want the "Tina Turner" reply. I bite my tongue to keep from asking him why he looks so tense and can't just relax. It would have felt so rewarding.

"Why are all these people in line? Are they going to see Tina Turner with us?" she asks as we join the long queue for security screening.

"Mom," I hiss, "You have to stop saying the Tina Turner thing. Bobby doesn't like it." It's strange that she can remember that part of it, but not that her grandson is getting married. "Now just be quiet and help me get your shoes off."

"Why in the world would I want to take my shoes off?" she asks indignantly, giving me a look that says she thinks I have finally lost it.

"It's just what you have to do now before you can get on an airplane. Just be glad you're in the wheelchair and don't have to walk through barefoot like the rest of us."

"They won't let you wear shoes on an airplane?" she sounds genuinely puzzled.

"It's just to make sure that you don't have anything hidden in your shoes," Bob pipes up, sensing my frustration.

"I really have to go to the bathroom," she says.

Oh no, I think, *Not now.* "Well, just hold on a few minutes until we're through with this ordeal and I'll take you."

The security man is beckoning us forward, and Bob pushes the wheelchair through, while I help Mom walk through the screening tunnel with her cane. The scanner rings loudly and they ask her to remove her shoes after all. The scanner rings again.

"Do you have an artificial hip?" the man asks her.

"Oh, no these hips were dealt to me by my creator," she replies jauntily.

"Yes, yes, she does! She has an artificial hip replacement." I am almost shouting.

She looks at me with a scornful expression. "Sherry, I certainly do not."

By this time, the TSA man is handing us off to a female associate for a personal search and they are both eyeing me suspiciously. *Are they thinking perhaps I have hidden liquid explosives in Mollie's underwear?* Bob gives me the first of many sympathetic looks on the trip, as I tag along behind her to the "private" screening area, which isn't private at all.

The female TSA agent runs a wand up and down both sides of her body, making her spread her legs like a common criminal. As she reaches the inside of her legs, Mollie quips, "It's been a long time since anyone did that to me." She smiles and rolls her eyes for the benefit of the on-looking travelers. She is giggling and seems to be thoroughly enjoying all the attention.

"Do you have an artificial hip replacement?" the woman asks with a serious tone that I find alarming. As I start to answer for Mom, the attendant shushes me with an angry wave of her hand. Mom is beginning to pick up on the gravity of the moment and says in a quiet whisper, "I don't think I do, but my son would know." The lady waves Bob over, totally ignoring me. "Does your mother have an artificial hip?" she asks brusquely.

"Yes, she does."

"Why did she say she didn't?" she queries him like a detective on CSI.

"She has Alzheimer's disease, and she can't remember things," Bob answers quietly.

"Bobby. Why would you say such a thing?" Mollie says.

At that point, the lady waves us through and turns her attention to harassing some poor woman with a baby and toddler in tow.

Bob pushes the wheelchair to a bench where I jostle Mollie's shoes back on. We are all pretty quiet and subdued at that point, and we head for the shuttle.

"I really have to go to the bathroom," she murmurs again. Bob stops outside the Ladies Room, and I help her out of her chair and into the handicapped stall.

"Why did Bobby say such a mean thing about me?" she asks.

"What did he say, Mom?"

"Well, I can't exactly remember, but I think he hurt my feelings." she looks confused.

"I'm sure he didn't mean to," I say. I really feel sorry for her, although at that point I feel sorrier for myself.

We are allowed to board the plane first and Mom keeps exclaiming how lovely it is and asking Bob if he had remodeled it. At least she isn't asking about Tina Turner anymore. We get her settled in the middle between us and just as the stewardess is finishing up her emergency procedures spiel, Mom says quite loudly, "I really have to pee."

Oh no, not again. "Mom, the plane is getting ready to take off; you have to wait until we're in the air. Besides," I whisper, "you're wearing a pad so if you have a little accident, it won't matter."

"I have to pee," she says in a panicked tone.

When we are finally airborne, Bob and I manage to get her on her feet after several tries, and I help her down the aisle to the bathroom in front, which seems to be a million miles away. I manage to get her in the door while I stand outside as a sentinel. I try to hold the door slightly closed, but she pulls it hard and it slams with a bang. I feel as though everyone in the plane is staring at me. I look at Bob, and he is giving me another sympathetic look. Once again, Kathy's admonishment is sounding loudly in my ears.

The balance of our trip goes pretty smoothly. Mom seems to feel secure in her seat between the two of us. She only asks a few more times where we are going and by just shushing her, we manage to avoid Tina Turner. I am hoping she will forget about it completely.

We wait until almost everyone has deplaned before getting her on her feet and out of the cabin. We find a wheelchair outside the plane and make our way to baggage claim. My daughter Tammy calls and says she is running a little late, but she picks us up about fifteen minutes later. When she walks in, Mom recognizes her immediately and they hug each other repeatedly. Tammy is Mollie's eldest granddaughter and they have always had a special bond. I am now so happy we brought Mollie.

We are finally on our way to Mollie's youngest daughter, Kristie's house, where she will stay, while Bob and I will be staying in Tammy's upstairs bedroom

As soon as we get in the car, Mom says, "Now, tell me again where we're going."

"Well, you are going to stay with Kristie and Daniel and we are going to stay with Tammy," I reply.

"Who is Kristie, again?" Mom asks.

"She's your youngest daughter. You remember pretty Kristie."

Tammy gives me a look that says, "Wow, she doesn't remember Kristie anymore."

As we are on our way to Kristie's house I realize that we will be passing directly in front of Mom's old house. I wonder if she will recognize it and say anything. We drive by the house and Mom doesn't even cast a look at it. She has no recollection of the last home she shared with her husband. This makes me feel sad for her.

Bob and I exchange glances, and Tammy just shakes her head. Mollie lived in that house for over four years with her husband Bob, and then Mary lived there with them for three years, and the sight of it doesn't even register with her.

As we pull up in front of Kristie's house, Mom is just starting to ask us who lives here when Kristie bursts out of the door. Mom smiles with recognition and I breathe a sigh of relief for both her and Kristie. At least she knows her youngest child when she sees her and they cheerfully embrace.

We visit with Kristie for a little while and then get up to leave. Mom looks confused.

"You're not leaving without me are you?" she asks Bob.

"You are going to stay with Kristie until after the wedding and then we'll all go home together," he reassures her.

"Oh, who's getting married?"

"Brett's getting married," says Kristie before we can head her off.

"Little Brett, who's he marrying?"

"Tina," answers Kristie.

"Tina Turner?" we all ask in unison and then we burst out laughing. Mom looks even more confused.

As we drive away from the house, I feel a sense of euphoria. I feel free. I feel as though a burden has been lifted from my shoulders. I try to feel guilty for those feelings, but it just won't come. It has been over two and one-half years that I have felt completely responsible for Mollie, and now just for the next few days, it's someone else's job. I feel almost giddy. That night when we go out to dinner with my daughter's family, I don't have to get anyone ready but myself. I feel liberated.

The next day, Kristie calls. "We had a terrible night," she says. "I slept on the couch outside Mom's bedroom door. She cried half the night. She didn't know where she was; she was afraid she would wet the bed; and she thought Bobby and you had left her.

I think it was downright cruel to bring her to this darn wedding. It's just plain mean to put someone with her condition through such a terrible ordeal. I finally just crawled in bed with her and held her. I didn't sleep a wink all night."

I feel terrible. I had thought this would be something that Mom would enjoy, but maybe I was wrong. Maybe Kathy and Kristie were right. Maybe subjecting Mom to all this confusion was somehow unkind. I had told myself that she would enjoy seeing so many of her relatives and that we owed it to Mary and Brett to bring her to this wedding, but maybe I was the one who wanted to come and I was using Mom as an excuse. Maybe I had just been thinking of myself.

"Do you want me to come over there and stay?" I ask.

Kristie's tone softens a bit, "No, the wedding's tomorrow, so we only have a couple days to go; maybe it will get better."

The day of the wedding starts off beautifully. The wedding is being held at Brett's family's farm on the banks of the French Broad River. It is a warm day in May and it is abundantly apparent that spring has come to Tennessee. The dogwoods are in full bloom, the irises compete with them in showy elegance, and the daffodils show their approval with brilliant yellow heads nodding in the gentle breeze.

When we arrive at the farm, I see that tents have been set up for the reception and a makeshift altar has been set up right next to the water. It is covered with white daisies and roses and wrapped in sheer white tulle. The rows of chairs stretch out in front of it and I can see that the gently swirling river will be a beautiful backdrop for the ceremony. The new leaves on the river birch trees, with their distinctive peeling bark, are fluttering and gently glimmering in the sun. The setting could not be more picturesque.

Bob and I are seated about three rows back next to our children and grandchildren. I look over at my immediate family with great pride and love. My husband is very handsome in his suit, his neatly trimmed white beard conveying a look of wise maturity. My dark-haired daughters are stunningly beautiful. Tammy's tall husband, Tom, still towers above his three strapping sons, but not by so much anymore; and their daughter, Anna, is creeping up on the blush of teenage years. Jennifer's daughter, Tova, is a Dresden miniature of her mother, and little Desmond could be the poster child for what a three- year-old boy should look like, with his dark curls and big blue eyes.

My life has been so blessed, and I think about how sad it would be not to remember this moment in my later years. Memories are such an integral part of who we are. Any one of us could be afflicted with Mollie's disease as we age. What a horrible fate she has suffered. My thoughts turn to Mollie and I wonder how she is coping, and how her mind is interpreting this event

Just then, Kristie and her husband Daniel, and their two children come to take their seats. Mollie is being gently guided down the aisle on Daniel's arm. She looks lovely in her powder blue suit, and I notice that Kristie has washed and set her hair. She is such a handsome older woman and I feel a surge of love for her. Kristie looks a little harried, but she is beautiful as always. She gives me a weak smile and rolls her eyes. I feel a bit sorry for her. I wonder if Mom is still on the "Tina Turner merry-go-round."

Brett's sisters Camille and Hannah come back and take Mom up to the front row to sit with them, next to their paternal grandfather. She looks around in confusion and catches my eye.

"Sherry," she says, "what are you doing here? Oh, I'm so glad you and Bobby could make it."

I smile at Bob. She obviously doesn't remember our infamous plane ride, and I wonder what is going through her mind. Does she think she still lives here? Does she even know where "here" is? It's hard to gauge the extent of her confusion. But I try to banish those thoughts and enjoy the moment.

The ceremony is picture perfect. My greatest wish at the moment is that Mary could have lived long enough to be a witness to her son's happiness: Brett marrying his childhood sweetheart in the most beautiful setting imaginable, bringing happiness to two people, who had suffered too many losses for ones so young. Just as the vows are completed and the sun is starting to make its fiery descent over the river, two beautiful doves fly overhead. They appear to circle the wedding party and dip low before flying off over the water.

Mary and Evan? I wonder.

The reception takes place on the same grounds as the wedding. As I mingle with Brett's family, I am surprised to hear so many of them comment on the doves. They all attached the same symbolism to their appearance and somehow I felt that Brett's mother had been there after all.

We enjoy another two days with family after the wedding and then we fly back to Florida. The return trip is much less eventful. Over all, I'm glad for everyone's sake that we brought Mollie to the wedding.

However, I will never hear a Tina Turner song again without remembering our trip

CHAPTER 28

You Say Potato and I Say Potahto
Let's Call the Whole Thing Off
George and Ira Gershwin – 1936

PRIOR TO MOLLIE'S living with us; our daughter Tammy's youngest children would come in the summer and spend several weeks. This was a big help to her because she didn't have to make other arrangements for the younger kids while she worked. Bob and I enjoyed having them and tried to do fun things with them during their visit. We chose to forgo their visit during the first summer Mollie was here. This year, we are determined that it will be a good thing for all of us.

Tammy and family are driving down from Tennessee and will spend a few days with us before returning home, after leaving Sam and Anna. I am really excited. I have not seen them since the wedding in the spring. I have instructed them to plan on having dinner when they arrive. Bob is putting his hallmark special touches on the yard and beachside, (he even rakes the swimming hole) and I sense his excitement as well.

"I just don't know how I can get this celery chopped and the potato salad made," I say, more to myself than anyone else. "I still have to run to the store, and the kids will be here around six o'clock."

"Sherry, I don't know why you won't let me make the potato salad," Mom whines. She is sitting at the kitchen table, trying to do a crossword puzzle (which still amazes me.) She likes to sit in the kitchen when I am preparing meals, and she always offers to help. I have learned that her help is usually not a help, but rather, a hindrance...but maybe this time.

"Well," I think to myself, "She always made better potato salad than I did anyway. Besides, I always faulted Mary for not allowing her to do things to feel useful. What harm could there be to let her try? Bob will be here to keep an eye on her and make sure she doesn't hurt herself. Go for it."

"I think that's a good idea, Mom. You were always the queen of potato salad." I smile broadly at her and she basks at my compliment.

I set her up with the celery, knife and cutting board. I chop one stalk and put it in the bowl to remind her of what she's supposed to do. "Okay," I say, leaping in feet first. "The eggs are boiling, and here's the mayo, onion, and relish." I assemble all the ingredients that she always used in her potato salad recipe. The potatoes are already draining in the colander.

Mollie is so happy. She is beaming like a little girl who just won the spelling bee. She seems so proud to be trusted with a task. I begin to wonder if I have been wrong all along by trying to do everything for her. At this moment, she seems so normal and capable.

I grab my purse and head for the door after giving her a little peck on the cheek. I find Bob driving around in the golf cart, picking up Spanish moss that has fallen. I explain what Mom is doing and ask him to keep an eye on her.

"Do you really think she'll be able to do that?" He seems a bit nervous.

"I don't think we give her enough chances," I say with my newfound clarity. I wave goodbye and leave him with his doubts. He promises to check on her often.

I arrive at the store with my list in hand. It takes me much longer than I intended, but I picture Mollie busily chopping vegetables and mixing the ingredients for her wonderful potato salad. She really is such a dear, and all she wants out of life is to be busy and feel needed. I realize that I have been wrong to deprive her of that feeling of usefulness. Well, I think to myself, this is a good lesson for me. I'll just give her more work to do, and we'll both be happier.

As I arrive home with my groceries and park the car, Bob waves at me and gives me a strange smile. I notice that he has made great progress on the yard, and I wonder if Mollie has been as productive in the kitchen. I walk in the house with two bags of groceries and high expectations.

Mollie is sitting in the family room watching the animal channel on television and I wonder if Bob tuned it in. She can't operate the remote on her own, so he must have set it up for her.

"How'd it go?" I ask.

"Oh fine," she says "Can I help you with your packages?"

"No thanks, I've got them. I'm sure looking forward to some of Mollie's prized potato salad, though." I say enthusiastically. She gives me a puzzled look and returns her attention to the family of prairie dogs on the screen.

I go into the kitchen.

The eggs are sitting in a pan that had obviously almost boiled dry. The celery is lying limply on the cutting board; uncut and looking almost obscene. The onion is nowhere to be found. The entire jar of mayonnaise has been dumped into the colander and is slowly oozing its way toward the drain. The relish, in lonely exile, is sitting in the microwave with the door ajar

The potatoes, however, are the *coup de grace.* They have been methodically lined up on the kitchen table like little soldiers; carefully arranged with the largest ones first, and the smallest ones at the end of the line. Some have been peeled and some have not. The head potato, which has not been peeled, has a nose, eyes and mouth cut into him; and he is wearing a little celery leaf placed at a jaunty angle on the top like a sporty fedora.

In spite of myself, I am amused.

"What happened to the potato salad?" I shout to Mollie.

"Oh, I love potato salad," she hollers back. "Can I help you make it?"

CHAPTER 29

You Make Me Feel So Young
Frank Sinatra – 1946

WATCHING THE GRANDKIDS relate to Mollie is great fun. She gets right down on their level, and as I go about the house, I frequently hear them giggling. Sam, who at fifteen is the youngest of three boys, seems to enjoy her the most. This gawky man-child is the apple of my eye. He is a tall, slender boy with dark, penetrating brown eyes fringed with long black lashes. He has a kind and gentle soul and has acquired a special attachment to Mollie.

Anna, who is eleven and the only daughter in Tammy's family, has always been good at entertaining herself; but even at that, she loves to hear stories about Mollie's childhood, and she will sit on the floor in front of Mollie's chair and listen attentively. The children are really quite good companions to her.

In the short time they have been visiting, she has taught them all her silly little songs and they sing them together at the top of their voices. Mollie picks out the tune on either the piano or her ukulele. I envy their playfulness and uncomplicated relationship. I always seem to feel the need to teach them little life lessons and not just enjoy them the way Mollie does.

All of the kids and grandchildren have always loved Mollie. She makes time for them and she acts as goofy as they do. She will sit and play board games or cards with them; and even though they have to keep reminding her of what she is doing, they are very kind and gentle with her.

She also likes to play croquet out in the yard. "Sammy I bet I can beat you at that yard game we play," she challenges.

"No way, I can even beat Pop Pop," he counters. But I notice that he always gives her pointers on how to hit the ball and which wicket she should aim for; and although his teen-age machismo won't quite allow him to lose, he doesn't play his best either.

Having the children here has actually made my job seem a little easier. We have planned to take the kids to Discovery Cove to spend the day and also to swim with the dolphins. We had thought we would ask Kathy to stay with Mom, but now I ask the kids if they think she should go with us, and both give an enthusiastic thumbs-up. When we arrive at the park, they supply us a wheelchair with large oversized balloon tires. A normal wheelchair would be impossible to maneuver because the entire grounds are covered with fine white beach sand.

When our time for the dolphin encounter arrives, Bob and the children and I don life vests and are issued snorkels and goggles. We position Mom's wheelchair in a shaded spot close to the lagoon, so that she can see and hear us. She is very excited.

When the trainer shows the children the command to make the dolphin jump out of the water, Mom hollers like an exuberant child, "Go Flipper, Jump Flipper. You kids are so smart. That fish knows just what you want him to do." I think the kids are a little embarrassed, but the other onlookers think Mollie is adorable.

The day ends with a luau, which is held in a large tent. It features a hula dance with scantily clad girls in grass skirts. Mollie keeps trying to get Sam to go up on the stage and dance with them.

"Come on Sammy, give those girls a treat. Get up there and shake your heinie" Mollie shouts.

"Yeah, Sam," pipes up Anna. "Let's see what you got."

This is too much for Sam, and he bolts out of the tent, causing the people at surrounding tables to turn and look, which is the last thing he wanted.

Bob goes after him, and I admonish both Mollie and Anna. I wonder if Mollie will understand, but when Sam returns, she gently pats his shoulder and says nothing else.

When we leave the tent, Sam insists on pushing Mollie's wheelchair and I feel a surge of pride for him; although I notice he is decidedly cool to Anna.

Aside from this, our entire day is wonderful. Having Mollie with us added to the children's enjoyment and maybe even taught them something about compassion and understanding older people.

The misgivings I initially had about having the kids here while their great-grandmother lived with us have proven unfounded. It has been a delight to watch them interact with her and it occurs to me that this was a privilege that few have enjoyed. I reveled in having the chance to help teach them to cherish and respect their elders, and I try to show them by example.

CHAPTER 30

— ❧ —

What A Difference Day Makes
Dinah Washington – 1954

ALTHOUGH THE GRANDKIDS' visit gives me a distraction, the aggravating things that Mom does continue to torture me. I clearly remember having been critical of Mary when she was caring for Mollie. I would say to Bob, "I don't understand why Mary is so impatient with Mom. So what if she doesn't do everything exactly like Mary wants her to? What difference does it make?" Those words now haunt me because I feel exactly like Mary did.

Mollie still puts dirty dishes away in the cabinets and still takes wet clothes out of the dryer and folds them. I have learned to combat these actions by doing my chores before she arises, but my schedule gets a little out of whack while the grandkids are here. As I walk by the laundry room one afternoon, I see Mollie with a pile of neatly folded wet clothes. There are several drippy shirts, completely buttoned and sagging dejectedly from their hangers. I completely lose it.

"What in the world are you doing?" I shriek like a banshee, as I march into the laundry room. I jerk the shirts off their hangers angrily, causing them to ricochet around the room like deflating balloons.

Mollie cowers against the wall, as I snatch the folded pile of wet clothes off the table and throw them roughly back into the dryer, saying, "You're driving me crazy, old woman!"

She picks up her cane, straightens her back, and saying not a word, hobbles out of the room in the direction of her bedroom.

As my fury abates, I turn to see Sam. He is looking at me sadly, shaking his head from side to side.

"You don't have to be so mean to her, Mom-Mom, she was only trying to help," he says.

What have I done? I feel the hot sting of tears and a lump of shame in my throat.

"I'm sorry, Sam." I turn and head for my own room, but not with the dignity that Mollie has displayed; so much for my efforts to teach the children compassion.

The next day, she doesn't seem to remember the incident at all. Sam, on the other hand, gives me the silent treatment. I think about all the lectures I have given him about cherishing and respecting his elders, and about what a privilege he is being given to get to know his great-grandmother. I feel like such a hypocrite.

CHAPTER 31

If A Picture Paints A Thousand Words
Daniel Gates

ON THIS PARTICULAR day, Bob has taken the grandkids to see a movie, and I have stayed home with Mollie. Their visit is coming to an end, and I love to see Bob spend some one-on-one time with them. I have really enjoyed their time with us, but it will be kind of nice to get back into our old routine.

Mollie is settled in her chair, going through her photographs. She lugged the wicker basket out to the family room, and she is looking at them one by one, almost as though she has never seen them before. The ones that go back to her childhood seem to be the ones she loves and remembers the most. I find that I am able to go about my chores while she does this. I am taking full advantage of this and am around the corner in the kitchen, chopping vegetables for dinner.

While Mollie is looking through her photos, Oprah comes on the television. I brace myself for the comment that she always makes when she first sees Oprah at the start of her show. I am not to be disappointed. "Oh, don't you just love her little scrunched up piggy face? I think she's so cute."

I don't know where that comment comes from, but it is as perennial as the sun. I wonder if Oprah would have been offended by it. I don't think so, because I think Mollie means it lovingly. Oprah's show today is about child predators.

"Oh Sherry, have you seen this picture?" I come to see, drying my hands on a towel. I take the picture from her outstretched hand. The picture is an old black and white of a man in his late twenties or early thirties, holding a violin in front of him. He's dressed quite nicely in a long sleeved white shirt and dark trousers. He is quite handsome.

"That's my mother's brother, my Uncle Henry. He played the fiddle, and his half-brother, Grayson played the banjo. My sister, Vera was about twelve then, and she and Mom sang harmonies to their tunes. I was only about ten, and I just hummed along; but oh, they sounded good, and our little kitchen was so lively then. I didn't like Uncle Henry very much though…" Her voice kind of tapers off, and I see a strange look on her face. This is not the first time she has told me this story, and it always ends this way. It seems like she is hiding something.

I decide to pursue this subject a little further. "Mom, did he ever… you know, do anything to you that he shouldn't have done?" It's strange, but as I ask this question, Oprah is talking about how child predators groom their victims and make them feel as though they are to blame for whatever happens.

"Oh, goodness, that was a long time ago. I don't think we need to talk about it." She pauses and then adds, "Vera didn't like him much, either."

I persist. "Well, sometimes girls have uncles who take liberties with them; and the fact that it was a long time ago, doesn't make it right."

"Oh heavens, I don't think it was anything like that. And besides, my mother told me I had to be nice to him. Why one time he took a stool and sat by the side of the road playing his songs. I was so embarrassed. Everybody was going by gawking at my crazy uncle fiddling by the side of the road. I was mortified. Lands sakes, I didn't like that man."

She had told me that story many times before and she always showed such disdain for Uncle Henry. I couldn't help but wonder if he had been one of those "funny uncles" that many girls have. The type who pretended to be interested in little girl things, while all the while, he was busy trying to put his ugly hands up her dress.

I watch her shaking her head at the picture. "I didn't like him very much, but my mother told me I had to be nice to him," she repeats.

"Just how nice did you have to be to him?" I ask.

"Let's talk about something else. Would you just put this basket away for me please? Sometimes those pictures make me sad." She starts singing an old gospel song quietly as I take the basket, and I know that our conversation will go no further, but I still wonder about Uncle Henry.

As I watch Oprah question actual child predators, I keep thinking about Mollie's uncle and wondering if those things happened in the olden days. Surely, human nature was the same as it is now. I guess it just wasn't talked about. I wonder if that explains why Mollie seems to have a preoccupation about sexual things.

She always drops little innuendoes, usually directed at my relationship with Bob. Once when Bob said he was going to bed while Mom and I were still watching television, she asked, "Now, where does Bobby sleep?"

"He sleeps in the bedroom down the hall," I replied.

"Well, where do YOU sleep?" she asked.

My tone was definitely reprimanding, "I sleep in the same bed with Bob, just like you did with your husband."

"I'd like to see that bed. I'll bet it could tell some stories." She rolled her eyes and wiggled her shoulders back and forth.

I was always annoyed by those little comments, but I could never seem to come up with a proper response, so I just changed the subject.

Mom and I finish watching Oprah together and the only response Mom has to the segment in which the child predators were being interviewed is to shake her head and say she would never figure out how God could let such evil exist.

Bob and the children return from the movies and we all sit down to a nice dinner. Mom goes to bed fairly early, which is a bit unusual.

Bob and the kids and I go out to his garage and play ping-pong and listen to oldies on Bob's juke box. The kids especially love *Charlie Brown* by The Coasters.

The following morning I go into Mom's room to get her up. This is becoming an increasingly difficult task; sometimes taking three or even four "wake-up calls." I am surprised to find her sitting in her chair in her housecoat. I start to give her a cheery greeting, but then I see that she is quietly sobbing.

"Mom, what's the matter?"

"Look what someone has done. Who would have done a thing like this?" She lifts the trash basket for my inspection. There are hundreds of tiny little shreds of photographs. "Who would have done this?" she sobs. Her tears make her blue eyes glisten like crystals.

I'm aghast. "Mom, there's no one here but Bob and me, and Sam and Anna, and they never even come into your room unless you invite them."

"Well, somebody tore up my pictures. Why would anyone do that? They have no meaning to anyone but me." She is really bawling now and her nose is starting to run.

My mind is whirling. I knew that neither of the children would destroy her pictures. Why, sometimes they would sit with her for hours and listen to stories about her childhood and the people in the photographs. They would act very interested and dutifully ask appropriate questions. They loved her with an acceptance that I envied. They knew what those pictures meant to her, and they would never hurt her.

Could she have done this herself?

She is crying her eyes out, picking up shreds of photographs from the trash basket, and holding them lovingly against her heart. I notice that there are still quite a number of photographs in her wicker basket on the chest, so they haven't all been destroyed. Thank heaven for that.

"Mom, don't worry. There are still more photos in your basket and there were a lot of duplicates." I pick up the trash basket to take it away. *Once it's gone maybe she'll forget.*

"Let me go and get you a nice hot cup of coffee." I leave the room with the basket in hand. When I return with her coffee, she is still sitting as she was, but she looks a bit befuddled.

"Good morning sleepyhead," I say cheerfully, as though I am greeting her for the first time this morning, "Did you sleep well?" I am hoping she won't remember what happened.

"Yes, but I think I had a bad dream. I can't remember what it was, but I think it was a sad one."

Tammy arrives several days later to take Sam and Anna back to Tennessee. She agrees that Mom must have destroyed the photographs herself. She also remembers Mollie, her grandmother admonishing her to be careful about who she trusted. I guess we'll never know for sure about Uncle Henry, but I have my suspicions.

CHAPTER 32

——— ‰ ———

Tis Summer The Darkies Are Gay
From My Old Kentucky Home
Stephen Foster - 1853

IT IS THE summer of 2008, and Mollie has been living with us for almost three years. The presidential campaign election is in full swing with a bombardment of advertisements by the candidates along with the perennial debates and mudslinging. John McCain and Barack Obama are a constant on all the television stations.

Mom makes no secret of the fact that she favors Barack Obama, but she just can't believe that a black man might be elected president during her lifetime. The race issue prompts her to tell many stories from her childhood.

She is sitting at the table eating her eggs while I am unloading the dishwasher. She is looking over the newspaper and sees a story about Senator Obama. "Why I just can't imagine that a Negro might become the Pres-i-dent of the U-ni-ted States of A-mer-i-ca. Don't that beat all. My daddy is probably rolling over in his grave."

She puts down the paper and wipes her chin with a napkin. "Did I ever tell you about David Durham? He was a Negro fellow who lived near us in Smyrna, Delaware. He was just the nicest young man. Well, one day, I was working out by the lane in my mother's flower garden. I was about sixteen and David was about eighteen. He stopped by and passed the time with me, talking about his family's garden and how much he appreciated my dad lending him his plow. After he left, my dad came over to me.

'What did that nigger want, talking to you right in the light of day for so long?'

'Why Dad, he's no more nigger than you are,' I said.

Mollie always chuckled nervously when she told this part of the story.

She continues, "I thought my father would have a stroke. He rarely hit me, but I think he wanted to then. His face got redder than a beet and he started sputtering and…well, finally, he just turned on his heels and marched back into the house.

"Now Sherry, I don't want you to think badly of my family. That's just how it was in those days. Why, we were no better off than David's family; but we were white, and that made a big difference. We all were good God-fearing people. We all went to church, and we all prayed to the same God, but we went to different church-es. I walked right past David's church every Sunday, and I always thought they had a better time praising the Lord than we did. They sang such upbeat songs, and our hymns were kind of stodgy.

"Anyway, my daddy used to lend David his plow to use in his family's garden, so he didn't wish them any harm. He just thought they should stay in their place. But do you know what, when my father died, he left that old plow to David Durham. I still have the copy of the written note my dad wrote before he died. We were too poor to have a regular will, but my dad had a few possessions that he wanted to go to family and friends; and he wrote it out and left it in his Bible, and right on the bottom it said, 'I bequeath my plow to Negro David Durham from Frog Alley, Smyrna, Delaware.'"

As Mollie told this story, which I had heard many times before, I had always judged her father harshly, but I forgave him a lot when he left that plow to David Durham.

I remember Mollie telling another story from her childhood that involved race, and that she seems to have forgotten. This story also involved her father. It seems that a prominent man in their town had died and there was to be a funeral procession through the heart of the little town in honor of this gentleman. Everyone donned their Sunday clothes and went into town to pay their respects. Mollie was about six or seven at the time and she and her mother were standing on the side of the dusty road as the marchers came by. There was a contingent of World War One veterans in full regalia. There were band members from the school trying their best to play a funeral dirge on their beat-up instruments. Bringing up the rear were the members of the Ku Klux Klan carrying a cross and dressed in their white robes and hoods. Mollie said she had always been scared to death of them.

As they marched by, their identities camouflaged by their costumes, she noticed their shoes and then she noticed the feet of one man in particular. The side of his tattered shoe had a big hole cut in it to allow the protrusion of his big toe, which sported an angry red bunion. Mollie says that she immediately recognized that ugly toe and realized with horror that it belonged to her own father. She looked up and met his eyes peeking out of the holes in his hood and there was no doubt. She tells how she gave a loud gasp at this revelation, and promptly turned and ran home as fast as she could, sobbing all the way. She couldn't believe that her father would belong to such an awful group and that her mother would have no knowledge of it.

Every time she used to tell that story, her face would flush and I could feel her shame and discomfort. I wondered if Mollie's camaraderie with black people was some internal attempt to make up for the ill-treatment she had witnessed in her earlier years. I think about her story about meeting George Foreman and the delight she took in describing him, and now her obvious preference for Senator Obama.

I look over at her and see she is still pushing her eggs around on her plate. She picks up the newspaper and looks at the picture of Senator Obama and says again, "I just can't believe that a Negro might become President of the United States. Don't that beat all?"

"Well, if you think Senator Obama would be a good president, you can vote for him and make up for some of those injustices you talk about." I pour her another cup of coffee.

"I would, but I don't think they let people vote when they get to be my age. But, all those bad things happened a long time ago, and I'm proud of how far our country has come."

"Mom, stop talking and finish your eggs before they get cold."

She gives me a sarcastic little salute and starts to eat her breakfast but without much enthusiasm.

She seems out of sorts for the rest of the day. She just sits listlessly and watches television. She doesn't even take her customary walk or two to the mailbox. I hope she's not getting sick.

She has enjoyed good health the whole time she has lived with us, so I'm not too worried.

Actually, I have been a bit preoccupied with the details for our upcoming trip to Ireland. We have received our brand new passports, and I have purchased some new luggage and clothing. Kristie has agreed to come and stay with Mom, and Kathy is planning to take a little time off work to help her.

Bob and Jim, the husband of the other couple joining us, have talked on the phone about the perils of driving a rental car in a country that uses the "wrong" side of the road. Neither of them would ever admit it, but I think they are excited as well. Rachel and I have talked about some of the sights that we want to see. Every time we do, I feel my level of excitement ratchet up another notch. Neither Bob nor I have ever traveled abroad, so this will be a special experience for us.

CHAPTER 33

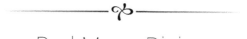

Bad Moon Rising
Credence Clearwater Revival -1969

THE NEXT MORNING I go in and awaken Mollie at about eleven o'clock. She says that she doesn't want anything to eat, but I cajole her into coming to the table and I scramble two eggs for her. She wrinkles up her nose when I set them down in front of her.

"Well, I know I'm not that great a cook, but they can't be that bad," I joke.

"I'm sorry, Sherry, I don't mean to hurt your feelings. I just don't feel like eating."

"Well, do the best you can. You haven't eaten since yesterday morning and you didn't eat much then." I leave the kitchen to take care of some chores. When I return, her plate is in the sink and she has gone back to her bedroom.

I check the garbage can to see how much she has thrown away, but I don't see any eggs or toast. I look in the garbage can again and see a paper towel roll folded up on both ends. I open it up and sure enough, the entire contents of her plate have been stuffed inside. She didn't eat a bite. I go into her room and she has crawled back into bed and pulled the covers over her head. I'm becoming increasingly concerned.

She sleeps the rest of the day and into the night. I check on her every few hours and even try to awaken her and take her temperature; but she complains that she is sleepy, and I relent and leave her alone. I can feel by her forehead that she has a slight fever, and I am becoming more and more worried. Maybe she just needs to sleep, or perhaps she has caught a little bug. Hopefully, she'll feel better tomorrow.

I check on her several times during the night and when I go in the next morning, she is awake but still in bed. "I don't feel very good. My pants are too tight and they hurt my belly." I press gently on her stomach and it is hot and decidedly swollen on the right side. I help her into a sitting position and try to get her to take a sip of water.

"Ooh, that tastes like gasoline," she makes a scrunched up face.

Bob has been urging me to get her checked out, so I say, "I'm going to call the doctor and get an appointment, something is definitely going on."

I am in luck. The receptionist tells me that they had a cancellation and to bring her in this afternoon. I let Mollie sleep, and then I help her dress and we drive to the doctor's office.

My worries about her abate a bit because she seems to thoroughly enjoy herself with the doctor. She sings some of her little songs while on the examining table. She is absolutely charming and even flirts with the doctor, who is only about fifty years old.

He points out to me that she is a little bit yellow, and he suspects a gall bladder problem. She is also quite dehydrated. He directs me to take her to the emergency room at the nearby hospital where they can perform some diagnostic tests, and possibly give her an IV to rehydrate her. I call Bob to bring him up to date, and we head for the hospital.

After an eternity of forms, questions and tests, they decide to admit her. They want to do a CT scan the following morning. As we are waiting for a room assignment, Kathy comes in. Bob called her and told her about Mom's condition. We wait for several hours and they finally take us up to a room. Mom has seemed fairly happy and chatty during the wait, but she really doesn't have any idea of what is going on.

There is another patient in the bed by the window and Mom notices her when we enter. "Where is this?" she sounds alarmed. "I'm not staying here all night, am I? I want to go home."

Kathy takes this one, "Mom, you know how your belly has been bothering you? Well, the doctors want to see if they can find out what's wrong, and they have scheduled a little test for very early in the morning, so you have to stay here." She barely finishes her sentence before Mom starts to cry. "Don't worry, I'll stay here all night with you," she adds.

I hadn't thought about that, but now that it has come up, I realize that someone will have to stay with her. She won't remember where she is or why she's here. Kathy is a head cashier at Home Depot and has a variable schedule.

"I have to close tomorrow night, so I can be here 'til about noon." She lowers her voice as she walks to the door. "You do realize she can't be left alone?"

I follow and when we're outside, she says, "When she broke her hip in Tennessee, she got hysterical whenever we tried to leave her alone. When they sent her to a nursing home for rehab, she tried to climb out of the bed. We had to go and bring her home at three o'clock in the morning."

"Oh boy, this is gonna be rough," my inner voice says; and I am ashamed, but I can't help thinking that it is less than two weeks before we are supposed to leave for our trip to Ireland. I leave Kathy and go home to update Bob, who has been anxiously awaiting news. I am hopeful that there won't be a serious problem with Mollie.

It's going to be awful hard on Kathy," he says. "She works full-time and it's up to us to bear the brunt of this. It's only fair."

"Of course, I know that." I am a little miffed that he seems to be implying that I should have stayed tonight. "I'll go back in the morning and stay for the test with her. I'll send Kathy home, but she probably won't go."

When Bob and I get there in the morning, we find Mom and Kathy in a tiny curtained cubicle. Kathy is trying valiantly to get Mom to drink a large glass of contrast fluid.

"I just can't drink that. It'll make me throw up," she is close to tears.

She brightens when she sees Bob. "Bobby, have you come to take me home? I don't want to stay here."

"I'll make a deal with you, drink this whole glass, take the test and I'll bet I can take you home tomorrow." he says.

"It's a deal," she says, and we have to caution her to take sips and not gulp it. Kathy and I look at each other in amazement: Male power at work.

When the test is finished, Dr. Goodman comes out and tells us that there are a number of stones blocking the main bile duct. He explains that he can probably clear them with an endoscope and that surgery shouldn't be required. "I could do this on an outpatient basis, but because of her age, I'd like to keep her in the hospital tonight and tomorrow night after the procedure. She should have very few side effects."

"Evil Sherry" is doing cartwheels, we can still go to Ireland... Oh and of course, "Good Sherry" is happy it's nothing too serious.

Bob decides to stay with her for the rest of the day, and I will come back and spend the night. The three of us spend the next few days taking turns staying at the hospital with Mom. The doctors don't give us any real reasons to be ultra-concerned, but they keep extending her stay. They tell us that it is just a precaution because of her age, but we all are becoming increasingly anxious.

CHAPTER 34

— ✿ —

When Irish Eyes Are Smiling
Bing Crosby - 1939

"WHAT THE HELL do you mean; you don't think we should go?" I spew the words out incredulously, even though I have been expecting them for days. Bob and I are sitting in his workshop enjoying a glass of wine, after having both taken our turn at the hospital with Mollie. Kathy will be staying there tonight since she doesn't go in to work until nine o'clock in the morning. This will be the sixth night of Mollie's hospital stay. The doctor has told us that he was not able to clear all of the stones lodged in the duct and he wants to observe her to see if more endoscopic surgery is warranted.

"Sherry, you know that's the right thing to do, and I can't understand why you won't..."

I cut him off midsentence. My voice sounds whiney even to me. "Bob, you can't do this. We have been planning this trip for months. Everything is taken care of. Kristie is coming day after tomorrow to take care of your mother, and I doubt that she will be in the hospital much longer anyway. You are just looking for an excuse not to go. You never wanted to in the first place, and now you're using this as an excuse."

I jump up from my chair, knocking my glass of wine to the floor where it shatters... like my dreams of going to Ireland. I know in my heart that he will win this one. I also know that he is right. Damn him, damn him. I know.

He grabs my arm as I march by him on my way to... I don't even know where, just away from him and his "always do the right thing" mantra. I don't want to do the right thing. He pulls me to him gently but I struggle away and turn my back to him.

"I know you're upset. I know you don't think it's fair, but what if we go halfway across the world to Ireland and something happens? What if Mom dies? Can you live with that? I know I can't. If you insist on going, it's fine with me. I'm sure Jim and Rachel won't mind if you go with them alone. I'm sure you'll have a good time. Go with my blessings, but I am not going. I am not going to desert that precious woman in what could be the last moments of her life."

"But, she's not going to die." I plead. "The doctor says she's just having a harder time than he expected because of her age. She's not going to die."

I am sobbing hysterically now, and for just a fleeting moment, I see a glimmer in his eyes that tells me that maybe, just maybe he will relent; but it disappears as quickly as it came, and I know that he won't, and I know that he's right, and I know that I will not be going to Ireland this time either.

CHAPTER 35

---∽---

Oh What A Night
By The Four Seasons - 1975

I GET TO the hospital about seven o'clock the next morning. My spirits are low, but I have to laugh at the sight I see. Kathy is curled up in the makeshift bed we have constructed of two very uncomfortable, unyielding straight back chairs with very hard wooden armrests. Her bottom is sinking down in the space in the middle and her one leg protrudes through the armrest at such an alarming angle, I wonder if she has broken it. There must have been a nice nurse on duty because she has a pillow. I wish I had remembered to bring a camera. We could all have a good laugh after this ordeal is over. Mom would just love it. Kathy senses my presence and with some effort, maneuvers herself upright.

"Oh, What a night!" She moans as she stretches her tortured limbs. "Every hour on the hour Mom thought she had to pee, and I gave up on the nurses. I got them to bring in a potty chair that I could move close to the bed. They might complain about our staying here, but I think they're beginning to appreciate it. Thanks for coming in early. I really need a shower. I've been peed on more times than I can count. Mom gets panicky and goes before she gets on the seat. She's not much different this morning than yesterday. She still can't keep anything down, and she is still constantly belching."

I go over to Mom's bed. She is sleeping soundly, and I guess the medication is allowing that. I had thought she was being over-medicated, but I guess she's comfortable. While Kathy is gathering up her stuff, I go down to the end of the hall and get a cup of coffee. Bob is planning to come in at three, and I am going to come back about nine and spend tonight so Kathy can have a break. I think she is trying to do more than her share, and we always argue about who will spend the night, but I think I can persuade her. This is becoming the new normal for us.

After Kathy leaves, I go over to Mom's bedside. I take her hand and hold it to my cheek, willing her to open her eyes and smile, but to no avail. She's still on the IV, but I have high hopes that maybe I can get her to eat something today. I'm going to ask them to back off a little on the medication. Dr. Goodman had hoped the first procedure would have worked better, but now he tells us that there may have to be another one, and unfortunately, the pancreas (which I have learned is the temperamental diva of the body) has begun to attack itself and try to self-destruct. They are waiting a few days, in the hopes that it will calm down.

The nurse comes in about eight o'clock to give Mollie injections. I ask her if we can hold off until after I talk to the doctor. I'm hoping it will be Dr. Goodman today and not Dr. Lesser (Kevorkian to Kathy and me). Mrs. Cohen, the lady in the opposite bed from Mom hears us talking about him and starts laughing when we call him that. She is supposed to go home today, but she has really been a sweetheart, and I will miss her.

I am in luck, because Dr. Goodman walks in the door several minutes later. He agrees that maybe holding off on the meds might make her more responsive, and more likely to eat or drink something. Sure enough, about ten thirty, she opens her eyes and looks around.

"Good morning, sleepyhead," I say.

She smiles at me and says, "I was having such a strange dream. There were two men and they were fighting over me. I think I chose the one in the Army uniform. He was pretty cute." She gives me a little wink. She seems more like herself, and I am heartened.

"Are you in any pain, Mom?" I'm concerned about withholding the medication.

"Of course not, but let me ask you, did my mom come in to see me? Has she seen my new baby girl yet?"

"Mom, you're so confused. You didn't have a baby. You're ninety years old, and if you had a baby your picture would be right on the front page of this newspaper and look—" I hold up the paper. "There's Senator McCain, not Mollie Turner." The lady in the other bed chuckles and Mom looks startled.

"Is somebody over there?" she gestures toward the curtain.

I pull the curtain back. "This is Mrs. Cohen, your roommate." I introduce them for the umpteenth time, and they smile sweetly at each other. I'm really pretty tired of sweet old ladies at this point.

Mom lets out a huge belch. I had forgotten that this was a side effect of the surgery. When she is sedated, it doesn't happen. Mrs. Cohen looks alarmed. She has been through this before, and I know she is happy to be going home.

I get Mom to eat a few bites of mashed potatoes and a couple sips of broth, but she soon vomits them back up. My spirits sink. *Will this ever end?* For some reason, the dietician had ordered spaghetti and meatballs for Mollie. *What the hell? Don't they read their patients charts?* I sent it back and asked for a soft menu. I was sure she would be able to keep it down. I am very depressed that she can't.

Bob comes in to relieve me, and Mom brightens at the sight of him. He is happy to see his mom awake and not in any pain, but is discouraged when I tell him that the belching and vomiting have returned. He's going to see about getting her off the IV. Maybe that is keeping her from feeling hungry. She needs to start eating.

An official looking nurse comes in. She is wearing a stiffly starched uniform, unlike the more casual dress of the floor nurses. Her hair is pulled back so tightly that her eyes seem to be elongated. There is nothing remotely friendly or gentle about her. *This looks like trouble, I think.*

"I'm glad that you're both here." *She looks anything but glad.* "I understand that you've been spending the night with our patient." She emphasizes "our patient" in a way that seems to trump "our mother." That is strictly against hospital rules. You won't be able to do that anymore," she purses her lips and straightens her back

"Well, you don't really understand the situation," says Bob. "My mother, your patient, has Alzheimer's disease; and she needs constant supervision. She might try to get out of bed to go to the bathroom, and she could easily fall. She can't remember things to answer questions properly, and that could lead to her being overmedicated. Her family needs to be here for her, and we intend to do just that." He is quite firm.

"She seems perfectly capable to me." she replies snippily. "Mollie, tell me your full name, please."

Mollie looks frightened, "I'm Mollie Elizabeth Bennett Turner and I was born on December 16, 1917." The nurse looks at us with an "I told you" smirk. "Now, tell me where you are."

"Well, I'm at my son's house." She points, "Do you see that television cabinet over there? Well, he built that right outside in his workshop."

The nurse looks disappointed, and without another word, turns and walks out the door.

Later that day after Bob has gone home, another nurse comes in. "I have orders to take out her IV." she says curtly.

"Oh good, maybe that will help her regain an appetite," I say.

The nurse removes Mollie's IV, and I feel as though this might be the first step toward getting her better.

The next day a new doctor comes in. He introduces himself as Dr. Martin and explains that he is filling in for Dr. Lesser. He flips through Mom's chart. She is awake and sitting up in bed.

"Why is this woman not getting an IV?" he asks accusingly. I explain that the consensus had been that removing it might encourage her to start eating.

He glares at her chart again.

"It says here that her son insisted that it be removed. Are you people trying to kill her? I can tell just by looking at her that she is dehydrated. In a person of her age, and given her condition, dehydration could kill her."

"Of course we don't want to kill her. My husband merely asked the nurse if the IV might be keeping her from having an appetite. He would never INSIST that it be removed, nor would I."

"Well, the chart says something different. The nurse wrote that the son was overriding the doctor's order. I'm moving her to intensive care to get her rehydrated. She could very well expire as a result of this."

I am really rattled by this event. I call Bob to tell him what's happened. He is furious. He remembers very clearly the conversation that he had with Nurse Ratched and how antagonistic she was about his query. It seems almost criminal that she would respond in such a manner.

The flip side to having Mom in intensive care, where the patients get one-on-one attention, is that for the next three nights, Bob and Kathy and I can actually all sleep in our own beds.

CHAPTER 36

A Pretty Girl is Like A Melody
Irving Berlin – 1919

AFTER THREE DAYS in intensive care, they move Mom back to another room. The doctors have decided that they need to go back in and try to clear more of the stones out of the duct. We go through another surgery, but it just seems to be a repeat performance of the last, except that Mollie is growing increasingly weak and is now sleeping almost all the time.

She has lost so much weight that her dentures no longer fit her jaw. I can't stand to see her without them. She was always so self-conscious about having false teeth; she even slept with them. It seems disrespectful to let people see her this way, and so whenever I am with her, I put them in her mouth, even though I'm afraid that she will choke on them.

She can no longer get out of bed to use the bathroom, and we have to get her on and off a bedpan. When Bob is there, he asks the nurses to do it, but they take so long that Kathy and I do it ourselves. This is especially difficult since Mom, who is very modest, still has a roommate. Soon it becomes apparent that diapers are the only answer. It seems so degrading.

Kristie has arrived from Tennessee, so now there are four of us to share shifts with Mom. Although Bob and I cancelled our trip, Kristie decided to come down anyway. We're all beginning to have second thoughts about Mom's prognosis, and I'm sure that entered into Kristie's decision.

One particular morning while I am there, an orderly named Ann Marie comes in to bathe Mollie, who is sleeping. Ann Marie is a short, fierce looking Jamaican woman with huge almond shaped eyes and skin the color of burnished copper. She walks with a gait that screams, "Don't Nobody Mess with Me." She's got attitude, and she scares me to death as she saunters into the room. I am a little bit concerned about how Mollie will react to her, given her attitude toward black people, and her lack of a verbal filter.

She places a sheet under Mom and begins her procedure with a gentleness that belies my first impression. She's talking to herself about the incompetence of the nurses for letting Mom develop a small bedsore. "They is nothin' but lazy. They should know that if they don't turn her proper, this is what happens. I see it time and time again."

Her tone changes as she speaks to Mom. "That's alright, sweet thing, Ann Marie gonna make it better." She croons as she applies some salve.

Mom's eyes fly open as Ann Marie is gently rinsing her face with warm water. I hold my breath hoping she doesn't say something inappropriate. She looks directly into Ann Marie's eyes and says, "Why, you have the most beautiful face I have ever seen."

Ann Marie looks up at me with a broad smile, "Nobody's never said that to me before." She just keeps shaking her head and smiling. She finishes giving Mom the most thorough bath she has ever had, and when she leaves, I hear her tell another aide in the hall what Mom said to her. After her shift is over, she comes back in to visit Mom and goes on and on about what a special person she is.

The next day when I come in to relieve Kathy, I find that we have been moved to a private room. Kathy says that Ann Marie came in and told her she was "gonna make it happen." Never underestimate the clout of a nurse's aide with attitude.

From that day on, Ann Marie never misses a day of visiting "Miss Mollie." On some occasions, she even brings her children. She is genuinely saddened to see her decline. Ann Marie's telephone number is now in my list of contacts on my cell phone and she has made me promise to keep her updated on Mollie's condition.

It is late September and I wish I could tell Mollie that Barack Obama seems to be leading in all the polls. I wonder if David Durham, Mollie's old neighbor, is still living and rooting for Obama like Mollie would be.

CHAPTER 17

—— ✙ ——

But The Days Grow Short when You Reach September

September Song
Frank Sinatra - 1946

SEVERAL DAYS AFTER Mollie's second surgery, two of her doctors have asked us to meet with them in Mollie's room. I haven't said anything to Bob, but I am very apprehensive about this. It has become apparent to all of us that Mollie is going downhill. She still is not eating or drinking. She has lost a great deal of weight, and she is now sleeping almost continually. I am hoping they will suggest some course of treatment that we have not yet tried. I know the others are beginning to worry about the eventual outcome, but none of us mention our fears to each other.

When the doctors enter the room, Bob, Kathy and I are all together. Mom is sleeping. The two doctors could not be more different. Dr. Goodman seems quiet, kind and subdued; almost embarrassed. Dr. Lesser is arrogant, confident and cocky. I dislike him intensely.

"We seem to have reached an impasse in your mother's treatment," Dr. Goodman begins. "The second surgery was not

213

successful, and the pancreas was further impacted. She is now producing phlegmon, which we have determined is solid and not drainable. We have exhausted all options. I'm terribly sorry to tell you this. I had thought the outcome would be much different."

Dr. Lesser gets right to the point, "Your mother is ninety years old, and we think it might be time for you to let her go."

What the hell is phlegmon? It sounds like a reggae musician and what the hell is he saying 'let her go'. He must be crazy!

I am shocked out of my internal rant by Bob and Kathy almost simultaneously nodding their heads in agreement, tears streaming down both their faces.

What's going on? I think. *They can't be buying this shit. We'll take her to another hospital, by God. We'll do it right now. We haven't begun to fight yet.*

I tune back in to the sound of Bob's voice. "The last thing I want is for my mother to suffer. She's an incredible woman, and it's been very hard to see her go through this."

Kathy has turned her back and is looking out of the window at the hospital parking lot. Her shoulders are shaking, but there is no sound.

Dr. Lesser persists, "When a patient is as old as your mother, they generally expire in one to two days once we take them off of any fluids or food. We keep them comfortable, and they are in no pain. Your mother has lived a good life."

"Expire...like a piece of chicken in the grocery store? What an asshole." I think. *"He has no idea what kind of life she has lived and what is he saying? - starve her to death? Let her die of dehydration? I can't be onboard with any of this - No way."*

I keep my thoughts to myself and after telling us that they will send the people from Hospice to consult with us, they turn to leave. Bob shakes Dr. Goodman's hand and thanks him for his efforts. Dr. Goodman pats him on the shoulder and walks out with his eyes averted. Dr. Lesser has already left.

The three of us are quiet and subdued. We don't look at each other's faces. Nobody wants to be the first one to speak. I am bursting with hatred for the doctors, the hospital …and even God.

I walk over to the side of the bed, where Mollie is sleeping. I take her hand. I wonder if she has heard any of this conversation. I read once that the hearing is the last thing to go and that people should be careful about what they say in front of their loved ones. I wonder if she knows that these two strangers have just given her a death sentence. Bob and Kathy have walked out into the hall, and I see them embracing before Kathy leaves.

Bob comes back in and stands behind me. "Sherry, I know you're not ready for this. I can tell by the way you're holding your body, but you need to realize that this is not about us. It's about Mom. We have no right to put her through any more torture at this point in her life. Think about what she would want," he pleads.

"Yeah, well, I never once heard her say she wanted to die," I respond feebly.

"Would you want to put your kids through an ordeal like this? You wouldn't, and neither would Mom. I need you to agree to do the right thing. I need you to stand with me, not fight me. God knows, this is the hardest thing I've ever had to do, and I need you beside me, and so does Kathy. You have no idea how important it is to us." His voice cracks and I turn and pull him close, inhaling the familiar freshly mown grass smell of him. It comforts me.

Later that afternoon, the people from Hospice come in and Bob signs the necessary papers to admit her to their care. It takes three days for a bed to become available in the Hospice House. Except for the nurses coming in to give Mom morphine, we don't see any hospital personnel. It's as if we've dropped off a cliff. When I ask the staff about this, they reply that once Hospice is in the picture, their responsibilities cease.

Ann Marie, bless her heart, still comes in after her shift, on her own time, to bathe Mom and change her diapers. I spill my guts to Ann Marie, and she lets me rant, and nods her head in agreement. I tell her how much Mollie has meant to me all these years and she hugs me. She tells me that she is sure Mom knows how I feel…I think that Mom was right: she does have a beautiful face.

When a bed becomes available at the Hospice House, I follow the ambulance with my car the few short miles to the facility. I call Kathy to tell her to come there instead of the hospital.

The first thing I think when I walk into the building is how much Mollie would have loved it. The inside looks like a nicely appointed living room. There are couches and chairs set up as conversation areas. A lovely rug covers the polished wooden floors. There are game tables and bookshelves laden with books and magazines.

At the rear of the spacious living room is a nurses' station adorned with fresh flowers, and at the center on each side is a huge hurricane lamp with a candle in it. I come to learn later that when a candle is lit, they have lost a resident. The candle on Mollie's side is lit and I later realize that it was for the resident of the room we will now occupy. I wonder how long before they light a candle for Mollie.

There are six suites on opposite sides of the nurses' station, where the twelve residents and their families pass their last days together. The individual suites are charming. They are painted soft colors, with a wallpaper border of roses at the ceiling. There is a TV and a CD player. The beds are covered with pretty quilts, and there is a pull-out sofa with fresh sheets and pillows and a huge soft recliner for the family to use. At the back of the room, a door opens onto a screened-in porch that looks out over a placid lake, framed by ancient oaks with drooping garlands of Spanish moss. I think how nice this will be for me and Kathy and Bob, compared to our sleeping arrangements of the last five weeks.

The Hospice creed is that death is just another phase of life on this earth; the final phase. It is to be treated with dignity and respect. They offer no medical treatment of any kind, only palliative measures to keep the person comfortable and make the process as easy as possible for all concerned. Every day, a team of two aides comes into the room to bathe Mollie and dress her in a fresh, pretty gown, not a hospital gown. Unlike the nurses in the hospital, these nurses are vigilant about administering morphine in a generous and timely manner.

It is a lovely place to spend one's final days and yet... I want some interaction with Mollie. I want to know she is here. I want her to ask me the same question over and over. I long for her quick wit and her hearty laugh. I need to hear her sing her songs again.

She lies almost immobile in this lovely room. She is always in a drug-induced slumber. She is totally unaware of her surroundings, or the constant presence of those whom she loved, and was loved by. She is here in body, but my Mollie is already gone.

CHAPTER 38

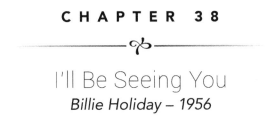

I'll Be Seeing You
Billie Holiday – 1956

ON THE THIRD day we are here, a gospel group comes to perform for the patients. Mollie has always loved gospel music; and I just know that when she hears this, she will awaken and even sing along with them. I open the door as wide as possible. *If she wakes up and sings, we can go home.*

"Listen Mom, they're playing *The Old Rugged Cross.* That's your favorite hymn. Listen to how well those singers harmonize." I sound almost manic to myself. There is no response. Please, God, Please. I'm losing hope.

The next day, I bring some Ella Fitzgerald albums that Mollie especially loved. I play them for hours on end, thinking that they might give her peace. I doubt that she hears them; and again, there is no response. After a while, I give up.

Bob and Kathy and I have been taking turns staying with Mollie around the clock for seven days now at the Hospice House. It is my turn and I am sleeping in the recliner up close to Mollie's bed, my head resting next to her arm, my hand on her chest so that I can feel each ragged little breath that she takes. I believe she is at peace. I am resigned now that the end is near. Mollie has morphine for her pain, but we must bear ours.

During the last six weeks, Mollie has been poked, prodded, scoped, stuck, debased and forced to drink obnoxious liquids to offer contrast to her inner organs. She has been bathed and diapered and had her modesty compromised by more strangers than I can count.

She's old and tired, and I believe that she is ready to go. At least that's what I now think. Mollie's dementia has kept her from communicating her wishes for her outcome. We, her children, are her advocates, her voice. We have spoken for her. I just hope we said the right thing.

I feel the grief rise from some wellspring in my body or perhaps my soul. It is palpable. It rises and expands until it lodges in my throat. It feels like a huge unhusked walnut; hard and sharp. It chokes me; it consumes me; I can't breathe. Then, mercifully, it releases its hold and pours from my eyes. It diminishes and I can breathe again. It is replaced by a feeling of deep despair.

It has been over two weeks since Mollie has received any fluids. I didn't think a person could live that long without water. The doctors all said it would be two or three days at the most. We are all wearing out. We have watched this good woman disappear before our very eyes. It's almost like she is melting and yet we've all gotten used to the way she now looks. She really is quite beautiful. Her cheekbones are so prominent and her thick, curly grey hair spreads around her head like a halo.

Kathy comes in about eleven o'clock. It is her turn to spend the night with Mom. I hug her when she comes in. She lets me, even seems to welcome it. Kathy and I have become kinder and gentler to one another. We have gained a mutual respect for each other. We each deal differently, but we each deal respectably. We have now been in Hospice House for ten days. I kiss Mollie on the forehead and head for the door and home.

I enter our darkened house alone. Our home, which usually seems to caress me when I enter, seems sad and foreboding, dark and unwelcoming, lonesome and melancholy. I have eaten nothing all day, but I am too emotionally drained and exhausted to even fix something to eat. I know that we are coming down the homestretch of this sad journey, and I am overwhelmingly grief stricken. I want another chance to be Mollie's caregiver. *Please God, I know I will do a better job if I can just have another chance.*

I'm too tired to even take a shower. I enter our bedroom, pull off my clothes and crawl under the covers next to my sleeping husband. I would love the relief that a good cry would afford, but I just can't. I am too exhausted to even cry. Just as I start to fall asleep, I picture Mollie's emaciated body, the deep hollows around the bones in her neck and shoulders, the sunken mouth and prominent cheekbones, and I wonder how I can still think of her as beautiful.

I hear a gentle movement around my bed. I open my eyes and there she is. She is dressed in her flannel nightgown, the one with the tiny rosebuds, the soft fabric puddling slightly around her feet.

"Mom, do you need something?" *I'm confused, why is she here?*

She lifts her long, graceful finger to her lips, and I almost hear a nonexistent shush.

She's just standing there looking at us. There is a soft, gentle aura about her. She has a slight smile on her face. She looks like

I remember her before she got sick. She's radiant. I want her to touch me, and I want to hold her.

I am jolted awake by the ringing of the phone. The clock on the night table says 3:33 A.M. *What? Where is she?*

Bob answers, "Hello."

"She's gone." he says.

We dress quickly, and drive the now familiar route. When we enter the darkened sitting room at the Hospice House, the first thing I notice is a candle flickering softly in the hurricane lamp on our side of the desk.

Kathy is pretty composed, but her eyes are swollen. I hope she had some time alone with her mother. Mollie looks so peaceful. She is covered with a quilt I have not seen before. Each panel contains an angel, and I guess this is the special quilt they place over those who have died. I kiss Mom on the forehead and hold her hand for a moment and then Kathy and I leave the room to Mom and her son.

As Bob and I ride home in silence, I notice that the moon is going down. I think about how much Mollie loved to look at the moon. How we would sit on the dock and watch the first traces of the full moon as it crept its way over the horizon. Mollie always was able to see the "man in the moon." As often as not, she would sing "*Moon over Miami.*"

On the way down our driveway, the day is dawning and there are two sand hill cranes in the yard, walking slowly, stopping to plunge their beaks into the ground, in search of grubs. The larger male, is protectively standing watch while his mate feeds. I remember how excited Mollie would get when she saw them. She loved that their little red caps looked like beanies; and she always noticed that their knees bent backwards when they walked.

When we go into the house, I see the watercolor that she painted of the dogwood blossoms and suddenly I realize: As many times as I wished that she didn't live with us; as many times as I was annoyed by her questions and repetition; as many times as I complained about her... I always loved her.

I know now that she will always be with me in everything I do. And in everything I see, I will see Mollie.

I'll Find You in the Morning Sun and
When the Night is Through
I'll be Looking at the Moon, but I'll be Seeing You.

Acknowledgements

DURING THE ALMOST ten years it has taken me to write this book, there are surely hundreds of people who have offered me encouragement and patiently listened to me prattle on about "my book." To all of you, especially my "walking buddy, Joan," I say a heartfelt Thank You. I would not have reached this point without you.

I am especially thankful to my daughters, Jennifer and Tammy, who bolstered my spirits and convinced me that my story was worth telling. They critiqued many drafts and helped make this a better book.

Many thanks to Michael Moran for taking Jennifer's concept for my cover, and whipping it into something I could be proud of. Your talents are incredible. Thanks to Julie Albright for the awesome photography, and my lovely models, Millie Sass and Jody Reeves. I can't wait to join all of you for another "Wine Wednesday."

I would like to thank Jamie Morris formerly of Woodstream Writers and the many workshop participants for convincing me that I was capable of writing a book. Your input was invaluable, and not only that, I think you all grew to love Mollie and her joyful spirit.

Thanks to Julie Albright and Joslyn Dunstan, who went over my manuscript with a fine-tooth comb and corrected many errors, and helped me not make too much of a fool of myself. You are both such diligent editors and good friends as well.

Finally, thanks to my wonderful, long-suffering husband, who always takes the "high road" and insists on dragging me along. With your love, I am a better person.

226